THE OBSERVER'S
POCKET SERIES

THE OBSERVER'S BOOK
OF
BIRDS' EGGS

THE OBSERVER'S BOOK

OF

BIRDS' EGGS

Compiled by
G. EVANS

Describing more than
ONE HUNDRED AND EIGHTY EGGS
With 154 illustrations in full natural colour
and 26 in outline by
H. D. SWAIN

With a foreword by
P. E. BROWN
Secretary, Royal Society for the Protection of Birds

FREDERICK WARNE & CO. LTD.
LONDON AND NEW YORK

FOREWORD

By P. E. BROWN

(Secretary, Royal Society for the Protection of Birds)

Whether we trap and ring, photograph or merely watch birds, we can cause them harm unless we take the greatest possible care. Few things are more vulnerable than a bird's nest with eggs and yet, to the bird, few things are more important—and to the bird-watcher, too, for if we want our native bird-life to flourish aboundingly, it is obviously vital not only that birds should breed, but also that they should breed successfully.

It could be argued that a book about birds' nests and eggs might be harmful, that it would encourage people to poke about for nests, to steal eggs and generally do damage. But almost everyone interested in birds likes to find a nest, and a book of this kind should help them to find it more quickly and to identify it without delay, so that the good it will do should undoubtedly outweigh the harm.

Certain cardinal rules should always be borne in mind by the nest seeker. Don't handle the eggs or disarrange the nest; don't spend more than a minute at the nest; don't disturb the natural cover or leave a track that other, less considerate, people may follow; don't visit a nest more than once in twenty-four hours. Never try to hunt for the nests of rare birds, for these should be left strictly alone.

5

Marsh Harriers have been known to desert completely following a single visit to the vicinity of a nest.

The majority of birds and their eggs are today protected by law, but they are also protected by a developing public sentiment. Innumerable people scattered up and down the land, in the suburbs as well as the country, get real enjoyment from feeding Starlings, House Sparrows, Blue Tits and other common but lively and attractive species which can be encouraged to visit almost any garden, and there are few people who do not find pleasure in the songs of Blackbirds, Thrushes and Skylarks. Our grandparents put birds' eggs into the drawers of a musty cabinet, shot highly coloured species like the Kingfisher to set them up in the parlour in a glass case where they slowly gathered dust and dirt, or massacred grebes and terns to embellish feminine headgear. (And yet, so hard do these barbarous habits die, that even in recent years the writer has had the unpleasant experience of sitting opposite a woman whose hat was decorated with the whole head and the red breast feathers of a Robin.)

Everybody who gets pleasure from birds should help to preserve them. The Royal Society for the Protection of Birds, with its headquarters at 25 Eccleston Square, London, S.W.1, is the national society responsible for the preservation of birds throughout the British Isles. For over sixty years the Society has been working for the better protection of birds through the establishment of bird reserves, the provision of whole- and part-time wardens, and through education in its widest sense. Man has it in his power to protect and cherish birds, which are as much an integral part of the whole scheme of Creation as he is himself. But he also has it in his power to damage and to destroy, and in few spheres has he done more harm than in his exploitation of the animal kingdom, with active selfishness and wicked indifference as the partners in crime.

PUBLISHER'S NOTE

Since the appearance of *The Observer's Book of British Birds* in the well-known " Observer's " series of pocket guides, the publishers have received many requests for a companion volume dealing with birds' eggs and nests. These requests have grown enormously during recent years, for in that time there has been an encouraging increase of interest in many branches of natural history and particularly in the birds of our islands. This in turn has led to a greater—although still very inadequate—interest in the protection of birds, and a corresponding decrease in such heartless acts as wholesale robbing of nests to satisfy the greed of the private collector.

There is still, however, a regrettable amount of egg-stealing, and this book has been compiled in the hope that, with a pocket guide to identification for use in the field which also provides a pictorial and, furthermore, a life-size record of eggs, the observer will be content to study eggs and nests in their natural surroundings—*and to leave them there.*

The eggs of almost every bird breeding in the British Isles are described and illustrated in this book. We must remember, however, that although general guiding remarks about their habits and behaviour can be made, birds are extremely individual in their approach. The times of nesting and laying, for example, are given at the head of every entry, but these are only broad indications, and some birds

8

may breed earlier or later. Unduly mild or severe weather can often be a guiding factor here and, of course, the habits of birds often differ from one part of the country to another. A further caution concerns the colouring of eggs. Those illustrated in the following pages are typical examples and, what is more, show the colours at their best. There is often considerable variation between the eggs of one bird and those of another of the same species, whilst many eggs become discoloured in the nest, mainly by damp stains.

Much is still uncertain or unknown concerning the habits and behaviour of birds, and if the observer can maintain a regular watch on certain birds and keep a factual record of what he sees, then he may be able to add to our general fund of knowledge. If this book can help anyone to that end, then part, at least, of its purpose will have been fulfilled.

Grateful acknowledgements are made to H. D. Swain, whose illustrations provide such a valuable contribution to the book, to R. L. E. Ford, who supplied the originals from which the illustrations were made, and, most particularly, to P. E. Brown who, in addition to writing the Foreword, has given freely and generously of his considerable knowledge and experience in the compilation of this book.

INTRODUCTION

A glimpse of bird's eggs in some tangled hedge-row nest is a memory to be treasured, and one cannot help but marvel at their beauty and at the work that has gone into fashioning the cup which holds them. The sight may prompt us to search for others, and to learn more about the birds themselves, but there are certain facts which we should always bear in mind.

The natural dangers to birds' eggs—chiefly steal-ing by other birds and by certain animals—are great enough without any additional threat from human beings, and we should, therefore, take care not to disturb the nest or alarm the parent birds unneces-sarily. Some, it is true, will never desert the nest, but others are easily alarmed and scared away.

Most birds have very little choice in the type of site, so that we can say, for instance, that Rooks always build in trees, Ducks near water and Larks on the ground, but this fixed nesting habit seldom means that the nest can be seen easily, unless it is in some place that is very difficult to reach. A few birds, however, have an extremely wide choice, and a particularly odd or amusing site is often pictured in the Press : the Robin and Blue Tit are perhaps the best known examples of this small group.

The pattern of nest building is usually the same within one species—sometimes even within one family—although a few birds may build anything from a very scanty nest to quite a substantial one—

Montagu's Harrier, for example. Generally, however, the pattern is varied only by the materials used. These are almost always provided by the immediate surroundings, partly for quickness' sake but largely to help in the all-important factor of camouflage. Here again, individual birds may provide exceptions —for instance, Rooks often travel quite a way for their sticks, and some birds will even select coloured plants or objects with which to " decorate " their nests, often making them quite conspicuous in the process.

The size and bulk of nests vary enormously, some being nothing more than a natural hollow in the ground, others consisting of an untidy mass of sticks and twigs, while still others are beautiful examples of intricate weaving. A very rough guide is that nests built on the ground, in holes and on ledges are usually rather sparse, whilst those built in trees, bushes, etc., are more substantial—but once again, this is no hard and fast rule, and there are exceptions, notably among the Ducks, which build on the ground but construct nests which are often quite bulky. Some of the scantiest nests are provided by shore birds, which make do with a mere scrape in the sand or shingle : one of the most beautiful examples of workmanship is the long, domed nest of the Long-tailed Tit—closely interwoven and felted, and lined with an almost unbelievable number of feathers. Such nests as this become all the more wonderful when we realise that the only tools used in this intricate work are the birds' beaks for collecting and weaving in each strand and fragment of material and their bodies for smoothing the cup into such perfect roundness.

When the nest is on the ground, it is almost always safe to assume that the young birds, when hatched, will be fairly well developed—not able to fly, but covered in warm down and with legs strong enough to carry them into cover. The more substantial nests built in trees, on the other hand, have to shelter young birds hatched in a state of almost complete helplessness—weak, blind, naked and dependent entirely on their parents for food, warmth and protection. Most of these nests, therefore, will have a safe and warm cup and many of them will be well hidden from view.

The development of the emerging chick also usually determines the size of the egg and the length of the incubation period. Obviously, the larger eggs, taking longer to hatch, will contain the more advanced chicks, whilst the less developed young will come from the proportionately smaller eggs after a shorter incubation.

The many species of birds produce widely varying numbers of eggs and also different numbers of clutches in the year. Generally speaking, if a clutch is destroyed it will be replaced by another, but a few birds—the Golden Eagle, for example—rarely lay replacements. Where the number in a clutch is large, it is usually also more likely to vary, and the eggs are sometimes small proportionately. In larger clutches, too, a common occurrence is one egg slightly smaller than the others and often noticeably different in colour and marking.

Most of us are familiar with the general structure of an egg, but how many know the reason for the tiny holes with which the surface of the shell is pitted ? They are the outer ends of tiny air-tubes which run through the shell to maintain a supply of air to the chick inside. The thickness of the shell varies a certain amount, but not in any relation to the size of the egg. Eggs of different species also differ slightly in shape. Those of birds laying in reasonably deep holes and tunnels are often almost spherical, for there is no danger of their rolling about. Plovers' eggs are quite sharply narrowed at one end, and this is apparently because they are rather large for the size of the birds, yet when they are arranged with their " points " inwards, the sitting bird can cover them adequately.

The different colours and markings of birds' eggs are a constant source of wonder and delight. The exact reason for them is not known, although camouflage is strongly suggested by the fact that many birds nesting in holes lay white eggs whilst those laying in open places usually produce the most heavily marked eggs. This by no means holds good, however, in every instance, and it is possible that the colouring of birds' eggs is to some extent still being gradually evolved.

There is, of course, no relation between the colour of the eggs and that of the adult birds—indeed, often the most brightly coloured birds lay the dullest eggs, and vice versa. Plain white eggs usually serve a purpose, for they show up well to the parent birds in dark places. Coloured eggs often have a ground shade which blends with their surroundings, and, where present, markings help in a dual way : firstly, by their pattern, which breaks into the outline of the egg—the well known principle of camouflage—and secondly by their protective colouring.

The markings are added just before the egg is laid,

and the sometimes curious patterns are due to the egg turning slightly as it passes down the oviduct. The difference in marking is great, but those on the eggs of different members of the same species usually show a distinct resemblance, though some birds—notably the Guillemots—provide exceptions. This similarity often extends to members of one family, which can sometimes lead to confusion unless the parent birds are identified. The eggs of each laying bird show the same broad characteristics of marking throughout her life, although each egg will differ in some minute detail and one in a clutch, as mentioned before, may vary greatly.

On the subject of colour we must remember Cuckoos' eggs, which show a very wide range of both colour and marking. They often resemble those of other birds, but curiously enough are not always found in the " right " nest for the similarity !

These are just a few points to note : far more can be learnt by personal observation, and particularly by regular watching of one particular nest—*provided only that the watch can be kept without alarming the parent birds or exposing the nest.* In recording our observations we must be careful to confine ourselves to facts and not, of course, to attempt to explain them in terms of human reasoning or emotion. Birds are creatures of instinct and habit, and although individuals may sometimes show what appear to us to be acts of human intelligence, we should not attempt to expand these, but should be content to accept birds as they are—interesting and extremely attractive members of Creation.

Those of us fortunate enough to have large gardens may like to set up some nesting boxes—and this is an excellent idea, for the spread of towns and industries has robbed many birds of their natural nesting sites. The most useful book on this subject, which is too extensive to discuss here, is *Birds in a Garden Sanctuary*, by C. P. Staples, R.N. It contains much helpful advice based on personal experience, and although we may not be able to plan as extensively as the author has done, yet we can adapt his suggestions to our resources.

CORVIDAE

RAVEN   February-March

Corvus corax

Ravens, the largest members of the crow family, breed in Scotland, Wales, Ireland and the western parts of England, particularly in the Devonian peninsula. In some areas they are almost common, and they are slowly extending their range eastwards.

Nest-building may begin as early as January, but will often be interrupted by severe weather. The untidy nest resembles that of the better-known Rook, but is very much larger, and is seldom built in a bare tree. Ravens prefer tall firs, cliff ledges, rocky heights or ruins, such sites being generally inaccessible. The building materials are sticks, grass, earth and the roots and stems of plants—varying with the locality, e.g., heather from high moors, seaweed from the coast. The nest is lined with softer materials, such as wool, fur, hair, moss, etc. Although it appears to be a straggling, loose structure, the nest usually stands up well to the often fierce weather to which it may be exposed.

The single clutch of eggs is laid in February or March and usually contains from four to six (or, rarely, seven) eggs, but occasionally there may be as few as three. The shape of the eggs is constant except for occasional longer specimens, but the colour can vary considerably. Usually the ground colour is bluish-green, freely marked with streaks and blotches of black or brown. The shade of green is variable, and the markings may be light, but all-pale-blue clutches are very rare; an occasional pink clutch has been recorded.

Raven　　　*Hooded Crow*

HOODED CROW April-May
Corvus cornix

The distribution of resident Hooded Crows is confined to the northern parts of Scotland, to the
Scottish islands, the Isle of Man and Ireland.

In structure and material the nest is like the
Raven's, though smaller. It is often placed on or
near the ground, among undergrowth on moorlands
or on a cliff site, but is sometimes found in a tree.

The eggs, generally from four to six in number
and laid in one clutch early in April, are smaller than
those of the Raven which they resemble. Variation
of colour is not great or common, and consists
mainly of paler markings.

Both nest and eggs may also resemble closely
those of the Carrion Crow.

Carrion Crow   *Rook*

CARRION CROW   April-May

Corvus corone

Carrion Crows are generally common and have a widespread and increasing distribution in England, Wales and southern and mid-Scotland.

The birds generally nest in difficult places along cliffs or in tall trees, but in districts where this type of site is not available they will build lower down, even in bushes. The nest is built of sticks and roots to which mud is added, and is finished with a lining of wool, grass or moss. It is a typical crow's nest, less massive than the Raven's and very similar to that of the Hooded Crow.

The single clutch of four or five eggs is laid in April and May. The eggs vary considerably in both shape and colour. The latter frequently varies even within one clutch, but in general the ground colour ranges through blue to green, mottled with brown.

CORVIDAE

ROOK   March-April

Corvus frugilegus

Widely distributed throughout the British Isles,
Rooks are common in districts with favourable
nesting sites.

The birds are sociable and congregate together in
Rookeries. These are generally built in very tall
trees such as elms, oaks and beeches but in some
country districts Rooks will nest in lower trees.
They do not usually select densely wooded places,
and often the Rookery will be quite close to human
dwellings—indeed, favourite sites will continue to be
used even when buildings surround them, as in the
centre of a town or city. The birds build or repair
their nests during March, when there will be much
squabbling in the trees, for Rooks are thievish by
nature, and ready to help themselves to material
from a neighbouring nest. Many of the old nests
become large and clumsy through constant additions
being made year after year.

The eggs, laid in March or April and numbering
from three to five in the single clutch, are very
uniform in size and shape, and elongated eggs are
not common. The colour, however, may vary considerably, and there are often differently-hued eggs
in one clutch. Colouring generally resembles that
of other crows' eggs, but the more unusual eggs are
olive-green all over, or have the markings greatly
reduced, leaving an almost pale blue egg. An even
more unusual variation is an egg with large ashy-
blue markings.

JACKDAW
April-May

Corvus monedula

Familiar and common in most parts of the British Isles, Jackdaws are particularly abundant in coastal areas and some towns.

They are sociable birds, though their colonies are generally smaller than those of the Rooks. Their taste in nesting sites is very variable : in country regions holes or crevices in cliffs, trees or ruins are used, as well as tree-tops ; but often the birds will come nearer to occupied buildings. They have often been known to attempt to build in an inhabited house, throwing sticks down the chimney and thus providing the household with useful kindling. Their lack of success sometimes annoys them, for they may take to throwing down rubbish with raucous screams. Where a crevice is used, there will be few sticks, the nest consisting mainly of lining material, but in a deeper hole, quantities of sticks will be thrown down to form a base for the nesting cup.

The single clutch is laid in April and May and usually contains between four and seven eggs. The ground colour is more blue than green, and the markings are much less heavy than in other crows' eggs. Unusual eggs are those with large black spots or with spots almost missing ; one extremely rare specimen had very fine scribble markings on it.

MAGPIE
April-May

Pica pica

Widely distributed and locally abundant except in the west of Ireland and the north of Scotland,

Jackdaw   *Magpie*

Magpies have enjoyed an increase in numbers with the decline of large-scale game-preserving.

They usually build their large nests in tall trees, choosing a fork among the upper branches, but will also choose dense hedgerows and thorny bushes, even when apparently suitable trees are available nearby. The nest itself is a bulky domed structure of twigs—thorny if possible. Mud is used to cement the lower twigs into a base, and the deep earthy cup is lined with fine roots and grass. Over this rises the " roof " of prickly twigs, with one entrance at the side close to the top.

The one clutch of eggs is laid in April and numbers from five to eight, although ten have been recorded. There is considerable variation in colour, the most usual form being bluish-green with small spots and flecks of grey and brown. The colour can range from dark olive-green to a very pale blue, with little or no marking, but the extreme variations are rare.

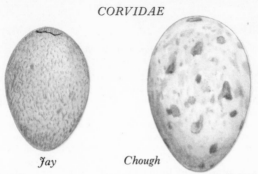

Jay   *Chough*

JAY   April-May

Garrulus glandarius

Jays are widely distributed throughout Great Britain, though rare in the north and absent from the north of Scotland. Like Magpies, and for the same reason, they have become more abundant in recent years.

Frequenting well-wooded areas, these wary birds build in smallish trees, in bushes or hedges. Favourite sites are often in tall thin saplings or in the shoots sprouting from the sides of large oaks. The nest is smaller than that of the Magpie, but less compact ; it consists of roots and twigs, and is lined with rootlets and occasionally with other finer material.

The eggs are laid in April or May in a single clutch of from four to seven. The colour is subject to a little variation, but is usually a bluish-green or greenish-buff, finely speckled with light brown, olive or grey. At the larger end there are often small scribble markings in dark brown or black.

CORVIDAE

CHOUGH April-May

Coraxia pyrrhocorax

Now unhappily among our rarer birds, Choughs nest only in western Scotland, western and northern Wales, in Cornwall (very few) and in the north and west of Ireland.

Fortunately the nests are generally inaccessible, being placed in a crack or hollow in a coastal cave or cliff, among high rocks, on an old quarry face or ruin. In a narrow space the nest may consist of little more than lining material—wool, grass, fur, etc.—but otherwise it is a fairly bulky structure, not unlike those of other crows, and consists of sticks, plant stems and roots, etc., with the soft lining mentioned above.

The eggs, laid in one clutch in late April or in May, have a creamy or faintly green ground colour, and are spotted and flecked with differing shades of grey and brown. Although these markings vary a great deal in density, the eggs do not appear to show great variation of colour. It must be remembered, however, that comparatively few nests have been examined.

Choughs may sometimes be seen in the same locality as cliff-nesting Ravens or Jackdaws, and the latter have even been known to feed with Choughs, which, however, are readily distinguished by their unmistakable red bills and legs.

STURNIDAE

STARLING   April-June

Sturnus vulgaris

Starlings are well known and widely distributed throughout the British Isles, but in the Shetlands and Outer Hebrides the birds are racially distinguished.

These abundant and familiar birds have a varied taste in nesting sites. In the heart of a town they will choose a gap in a piece of masonry, the protection of the eaves of a house, a drainpipe, a chimney, a large crevice in a garden rockery or a tree. In the country, a tree again may provide the site (holes which formerly housed other birds are not despised, provided that they are large enough), or a haystack, a barn, ruined buildings, a sandpit or a coastal cliff may be used. The nest itself consists of an untidy mass of straw and rubbish, lined with grass, feathers and any soft material.

The first eggs are laid in April in a clutch of from four to seven in number, and are a pale glossy blue, which fades easily to white. Starlings often have two clutches a year, usually between April and June, but sometimes they will nest and lay out of season. Occasionally you may come upon an egg laid casually on the ground ; more often half a shell will be found at some little distance from the nest, whence one of the parent birds has removed it.

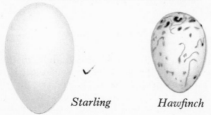

Starling   *Hawfinch*

FRINGILLIDAE

HAWFINCH   April-May

Coccothraustes coccothraustes

More often to be seen in the southern half of England and Wales, though absent from western Wales and from Cornwall, Hawfinches are extending their range northwards but are not found in Scotland or Ireland. They appear more common in some districts than in others, but are shy and secretive. They occur in quite well populated areas, even nesting in the larger gardens.

A favourite nesting site for these birds is often on a horizontal branch of a thorn tree, but orchard trees and tall bushes are also used. The nest, usually built at a good height from the ground, consists of twigs and roots lined with finer roots, hair or fibre, and often has an outer covering of lichens. It is a little larger than the nests of other finches.

The eggs, four to six in the single clutch, are laid in April or May; the ground colour may be off-white or pale buff, but is more usually of a faint greenish tinge, with irregular dark streaks and flecks strongly resembling those on eggs of the buntings.

Greenfinch   *Goldfinch*

GREENFINCH

April-July

Chloris chloris

Greenfinches are quite common and are distributed generally throughout the British Isles, including some of the Scottish islands. They are rather inconspicuous birds.

A good amount of cover is generally selected for the nest, which is built in overgrown hedges or shrubs, in profuse ivy or other evergreens, or on the flat branches of conifer trees. Greenfinches will often nest in largish gardens, in any suitable site in shrubberies, bushes or rose arches, but they like to be fairly well up, usually just beyond a man's reach. The nest itself is a rather loose structure of small twigs and roots, grass, moss and other fine materials, softly lined with hair, feathers, etc.

The eggs are laid in clutches of from four to six, the first in later April or early May, succeeded by another and perhaps sometimes by a third. Size and colour vary a little, the ground colour usually being cream or a very pale bluish-green, spotted and blotched with reddish-brown, purple or near-black.

GOLDFINCH   May-July

Carduelis carduelis

Fairly widely distributed in the British Isles, although completely absent as breeding birds from the north of Scotland, Goldfinches can most easily be seen during the autumn and winter months, when they feed in small flocks on burdock, thistles and other seed-heads on waste and poorly cultivated land.

In spite of their bright colouring, these lovely birds manage to pass almost unnoticed during the nesting season, but this may be largely due to the fact that they nest rather high up and in good cover. Orchards, gardens and farms usually provide nesting sites, a favourite place being at the top of a tall apple tree, where a convenient fork is selected, but hedges and bushes—usually of a prickly nature, such as thorn or furze— are also used. The nest is made in May, when leaves are all well out, and the actual structure is small and compact (not unlike that of a Chaffinch) and not easily seen. It is made from fine twigs, roots and grasses, interwoven with moss and lichens, and lined with wool, thistledown or hair, seldom with feathers.

There are four to six eggs in the clutch, which is laid in May and is often succeeded by another. The eggs are somewhat similar in shape and colouring to those of the Greenfinch, but are smaller.

FRINGILLIDAE

SISKIN

April-June

Carduelis spinus

Best known as winter visitors, Siskins are resident in some parts of the British Isles, chiefly in Scotland and Ireland, but they have nested in England and Wales, mainly in the northern counties.

Fir-trees and larches provide the favourite nesting sites for these birds, who like to build high up on a horizontal branch. The nest consists of dead twigs, particularly those covered with lichens, together with roots, moss, sprigs of heather, etc., and is lined with softer materials such as grass, feathers or wool.

The eggs are laid in clutches of from four to five, the first in late April or early May, often being succeeded by a second during June. The ground colour of the eggs is a pale greenish-blue, spotted and streaked with reddish-brown and a soft purple. There is a close resemblance to the eggs of the Goldfinch, although those of the Siskin are slightly smaller and have more of a bluish tinge in the ground colour ; the markings, too, are often more pronounced.

Siskins are frequently seen in the company of Redpolls, and sometimes with tits, in whose acrobatic feats they often share, particularly when feeding on the seeds of alders and birches.

Siskin   *Redpoll*

REDPOLL   May-June

Carduelis flammea

Very local in distribution, Redpolls are found in
more abundance in northern districts, often in
isolated localities.

They nest in trees, hedges, brambles or other
bushes, usually fairly well up, but the height varies
somewhat. The nest, less compact than those of the
other small finches, is built of twigs, grass, moss and
wool, and is lined with hair, feathers, wool and the
down from plants—often the fluff from willow
catkins.

The eggs are laid in mid-May in a clutch of from
four to six, and a second clutch frequently follows in
June. The ground colour is usually a fairly deep
greenish-blue, with speckles and blotches of reddish-
or purplish-brown. These markings are heavier
towards the larger end of the eggs, as in those of the
Linnet, which they resemble, though they are
deeper in colour and smaller.

Twite

Linnet

TWITE   May-July

Carduelis flavirostris

Twites are often called Mountain Linnets, for they frequent northern moors and uplands.

They nest close to the ground among heather, gorse and other low plants and bushes ; occasionally several pairs may build in one small area. The nest usually consists of small twigs and fine rootlets, interwoven with moss and wool ; the cup itself is small and is lined with any suitable soft material that may be available—down, hair, wool, and sometimes a few feathers.

The eggs are laid in clutches of from four to six, and there are usually two layings, the first coming late in May or early in June. The ground colour is a variable tint of greenish-blue, spotted and streaked with shades of reddish-, purplish- or nigger-brown. The eggs generally resemble those of the Linnet, but are often a little smaller, with a deeper ground colour, and markings not mainly confined to the larger end.

LINNET

April-June

Carduelis cannabina

More abundant and with a wider distribution than Twites, Linnets also haunt heaths and moorlands, but are not found in mountainous regions.

Their nesting time comes earlier than that of the Twites, normally beginning in the middle of April, and although they do occasionally build close to the ground, they usually prefer to nest a little higher—about three to four feet up. Gorse bushes provide favourite nesting sites, but hedges and brambles are often used, as well as other bushy plants, such as wild rose, particularly if they form concealing clumps against a bank, wall or fence. The nest itself is built of small twigs, stalks and rootlets bound together with grass, moss and wool, and is lined with the down from such plants and trees as thistles and willows, with hair, wool and a few feathers.

Laying generally begins in April ; there are four to six eggs in each clutch and usually two clutches in the year, although a third is sometimes produced. There is some considerable variation in colouring, the ground shade varying from a faintly bluish-white to a pale greenish-blue ; the markings, when present, are mainly clustered round the larger end, and consist of specks and blotches of a reddish- or purplish-brown, whilst further down the shell there are fainter spots. Often, however, there may be almost no marking at all, leaving a plain blue-tinged egg.

BULLFINCH   May-July

Pyrrhula pyrrhula

Bullfinches are widely distributed birds, apt to be
scarce locally, although their retiring habits may at
some seasons account for their apparent lack of
abundance. In summer they retreat to woods and
copses, but at other times they venture into more
open country, and may visit orchards and gardens,
where they sometimes inflict severe damage on the
buds of fruit trees.

Bushes, hedges and trees normally provide the
nesting sites and, like Linnets, Bullfinches prefer
to build well up from the ground, sometimes at
about four to five feet, but often higher and beyond
a man's reach. The nest is usually well hidden, but
when it is seen it is easily recognisable, as it is an
almost flat platform of interwoven twigs with a
shallow cup of fine roots lined with hair.

The eggs, from four to six in a clutch, are laid
first in May, and there is usually a second clutch in
July. The ground colour is nearly always a definite
greenish-blue, but there is some degree of variation
in the markings. In colour these range through
differing shades of brown to near-black, and are
generally confined to a zone of spots and blotches at
the larger end, with a few odd spots scattered on the
rest of the shell. These markings may, however, be
faint, or absent altogether or—in very rare instances
—may be found at the smaller end.

Bullfinch

Crossbill

CROSSBILL   February-July

Loxia curvirostra

Much less common than most of the finches, Crossbills are very scarce, for the only established breeding areas south of Scotland are in Norfolk and Suffolk. In Scotland they are, in a limited area, comparatively common in some years.

Coniferous trees are chosen as the nesting sites—pines and larches being commonly used. The birds vary their time of building, which may be as early as February or considerably later. The nest, placed high in the tree, bears a resemblance to that of the Bullfinch, the base consisting of interwoven twigs and the cup of moss, wool, hair, grass and similar soft materials.

There are four or five eggs in a clutch and usually two clutches in the year. The eggs are not unlike those of the Greenfinch, having a pale ground colour and markings of reddish-brown or near-black.

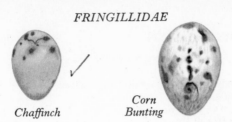

Chaffinch

*Corn
Bunting*

CHAFFINCH   April-June

Fringilla coelebs

Chaffinches are very common, being widely distributed throughout the British Isles, and most people are quite familiar with them. They appear to be equally at home in town or countryside, and frequent gardens, parks, orchards, woods and open country impartially.

A thick hedge or the fork of a tree is usually chosen for the nest, which is a small, wonderfully neat structure of soft materials like wool, moss, lichens, grass and—near houses—mop and duster shakings and household odds and ends such as human and animal hairs, string, cotton, etc. It is often felted over with spiders' webs, and the cup is lined with wool, hair and feathers.

The first clutch of eggs, numbering from four to six, is laid in April or May and is usually followed by a second in June. The ground colour is generally a dirty white tinged with any shade from pink to a brownish-red, but this may be absent altogether, leaving a pale greenish-blue egg. The markings usually consist of spots and streaks of a dark reddish-brown.

35

CORN BUNTING

May-July

Emberiza calandra

Widely though patchily distributed, but locally abundant, Corn Buntings frequent fields, open country and heathland. They are the largest buntings in this country.

The birds build in low bushes, in the undergrowth near hedgerows or even among long grass in an open field. A favourite site is in low scrubby growth along a steep bank or fringing a roadside. Although it is placed on or near the ground, the nest is very difficult to find, as it blends so well with its surroundings, from which its materials are largely drawn. Straw, grass, rootlets and moss form a rather untidy surround for the deep cup which is lined with hair, fine grass and other soft materials.

The eggs, which are larger than those of other buntings, are laid in clutches of from four to six in number. The first clutch is laid towards the end of May or at the beginning of June, and there is often a second clutch sometime later. There is considerable variation, both in the ground colour and in the markings of the eggs. The ground colour is usually off-white or cream, and is often tinged with pale purple or red. The markings consist of spots, blotches, streaks, lines and scrolls of various shades, ranging from purplish-red through brown to near-black; occasionally they are sparsely or erratically distributed over the shell, at other times they form almost an all-over pattern.

The song, often delivered from telegraph wires, is characteristic.

36

FRINGILLIDAE

YELLOW BUNTING April-August

Emberiza citrinella

Better known in some districts as Yellow Hammers, these are familiar and widely distributed birds seen on heaths, commons and open ground generally.

Like Corn Buntings, Yellow Buntings nest close to or on the ground, and in similar situations, particular favourites being low, dense bushes such as gorse and the hedge banks bordering ditches. The nest is a somewhat bulky but neat structure of grass, stalks, rootlets and moss. The rather deep cup is lined with fine plant fibres and sometimes also with hair.

The number of eggs in a clutch is usually three or four, sometimes five, rarely six. There are often two or three clutches in the year, and some birds breed late, chicks often being seen in the nest until September. Laying begins at the end of April or the beginning of May. There is a slight variation in the ground colour of the eggs from a dirty white to a very pale purplish or brownish tinge, but there appears to be no extreme of difference. The markings, however, vary a little more ; generally speaking they consist of fine lines and scribbles of a dark colour ranging from a deep purplish-brown to near-black, but sometimes the lines are thicker and spots and blotches are also present. These finely traced markings have given the species the various nicknames of Writing Lark, Scribbling Lark and Scribe.

Yellow Bunting   *Cirl Bunting*

CIRL BUNTING   May-July

Emberiza cirlus

Cirl Buntings are uncommon and are more restricted in distribution than Yellow Buntings, being found locally in southern England and in Wales, but rarely further north, and are seen only occasionally in Scotland and Ireland. They do not breed in Scotland or in northern England.

Cirl Buntings may choose similar nesting sites to those of the buntings already described, but in a bush or hedge the nest is built higher up from the ground. On the other hand, it may be found on a bank, often among the roots of a tree or bush. In general structure the nest resembles that of the Yellow Bunting, but it is a little more compact and there is usually a greater amount of moss used.

There are generally two clutches of eggs in the year, the first being laid in May. The eggs themselves are rather like those of the Yellow Bunting ; they may be rounder and slightly smaller, the ground colour usually lacks the warm tinge and the markings are bolder both in colour and in form.

Reed Bunting   *Snow Bunting*

REED BUNTING   April-August

Emberiza schoeniclus

The distribution of Reed Buntings is general, but their haunts are largely confined to waterside copses, marshes and fen districts, although in winter they may extend further afield.

The nesting site of Reed Buntings is always very close to water, among rushes and reeds, in a clump of grass or sedge, or in the stump of a willow. The nest itself is a well-built structure of any suitable waterside material—grass, sedge, reeds, etc., with sometimes a little moss added—whilst the rather deep cup is lined with finer dried grass, the fine beards of reeds and hair.

The first clutch of eggs is usually laid in April and contains from four to six eggs; two or three clutches are normally produced in the year, and eggs may be found as late as August, but the later nests often yield only three eggs. The ground colour varies from purplish-white to purplish-brown; the markings consist of bold streaks, spots and scribbles of dark purplish-brown or near-black, but they are sparser than those on the eggs of Yellow Buntings.

SNOW BUNTING

May-July

Plectrophenax nivalis

South of the Scottish highlands Snow Buntings are known only as migrants and winter visitors mainly to coastal districts. In the highlands of Scotland a very few pairs may breed fairly regularly.

The nest is usually situated deep in holes or crannies amongst loose boulders and stones in mountainous screes. Rootlets, dried grass, stalks and dried moss form the nest, which is lined with wool, hair, grass and feathers.

There is one clutch of eggs, usually four or five in number, but sometimes more, laid between May and July. The eggs themselves are a little larger and rounder than those of the Reed Bunting, and are quite different in colour. There is no great variation in the ground colour, which is usually white tinged with a dirty yellow, but sometimes the tinge is of a very pale bluish or greenish shade. The markings have less of the scribbled nature characteristic of the eggs of other buntings, and consist mainly of dark brown and grey blotches and smaller spots, interspersed with occasional streaks.

PASSERIDAE

HOUSE SPARROW   General, usually Mar.-Aug.

Passer domesticus

Very abundant and familiar, particularly in association with man, House Sparrows have a wide distribution throughout the British Isles, although in many areas they are very local in occurrence, being particularly sparse in some hill districts.

They choose a variety of nesting sites, often showing a preference for thick ivy growing on walls and trees, but they will also nest in crevices in trees and buildings, under the eaves of houses, or in trees, thick bushes and hedgerows. On occasions they will annex and adapt the old nests of other birds. In holes and in ivy the nest will consist largely of an untidy mass of grass and straw, plentifully lined with feathers, but when the nest is in a tree or a bush it is more carefully built, with a domed roof and an entrance in one side.

There are normally three clutches of eggs in the year, the first being laid in March, but this is only a very general rule, since there may be more, and eggs have been recorded as early as February and as late as Christmas. The clutch usually consists of from four to six eggs, but this also is variable, as too are the size, shape, colour and markings. The ground colour is most frequently a faintly bluish- or creamy white, and the markings are normally plentiful, comprising dots, streaks, specks and blotches of black, brown, and yellowish-, greenish- or ashy grey.

House Sparrow   *Tree Sparrow*

TREE SPARROW   April-June

Passer montanus

Although they have a fairly wide distribution, Tree
Sparrows are much more local than House Sparrows
and are considerably more timid. They are not
found in west Wales, in the Devonian Peninsula
or in south Ireland.

Most Tree Sparrows are sociable by nature, even
to the extent of nesting in small colonies in a disused
quarry or a clump of old trees—particularly willows
—but holes among rocks, or a hollow between the
roots of bushes are also used, and occasionally
crevices in old buildings. The untidy nest resembles that of the House Sparrow, but when, as sometimes happens, the old nests of other birds are used,
Tree Sparrows will build a firmer, domed nest.

The first of the two (rarely three) clutches is laid
in April or early in May, with from four to six eggs
in the clutch. Smaller than the House Sparrow's,
the eggs are generally browner ; the markings vary
in density and distribution, sometimes being clustered at one end, sometimes giving a uniform mottled
appearance. One egg in each clutch is often
noticeably lighter than the others.

Wood Lark

Sky Lark

WOOD LARK

March-June

Lullula arborea

Wood Larks are more commonly seen in southern and western counties and in Wales, but are only locally abundant and become more scarce further north, being seen but rarely in Scotland and Ireland.

Like their commoner relatives, they build on the ground, although they do not usually choose quite such open sites, but prefer to conceal their nests beneath a low bush or among other scrub, often near the shelter of some trees. Grass and moss form the compact nest, which is lined with finer dried grass and hair.

Laying begins in late March or in April, with three to five eggs in a clutch and two or occasionally three clutches in the year. The ground colour of the eggs is a creamy or greyish-white, sometimes faintly tinged with pale olive ; the markings consist of tiny close speckles usually reddish-brown, but varying at times to more of an olive-green. There is no great variation, although the speckles may be less or more dense, with sometimes a heavier band near the larger end.

SKY LARK

Alauda arvensis

Widely distributed throughout the British Isles, these larks are much more common than the last, although only locally abundant. Many of our birds are really summer visitors arriving early in spring and travelling south in autumn.

They nest in a hollow in the ground in fields and open country generally. The nest is very well concealed among the grass and extremely difficult to find, for the parent birds will never " pin-point " it, but will drop to the ground some distance away and scurry, hidden by the grass, to the actual site. Thus, even if you see the bird descend within a few feet of you, the chances are very slight of coming upon the nest itself. It is built quite simply of dried grass, sometimes with a little moss, and is lined with finer grass and perhaps a little hair.

The eggs are laid in clutches of from three to five in number, with two and sometimes three clutches in the year, the first being produced in April. The eggs are longer than those of the Wood Lark and often have larger markings. The ground colour varies somewhat, but is usually a dirty- or creamy-white. The markings are normally dense and brownish in colour, and consist mainly of blotches and mottles ; occasionally, however, they are smaller and lighter, giving a paler coloured egg. In rare cases there is a ring of dense markings near the larger end, as in some specimens of the Wood Lark's eggs.

TREE PIPIT

May-June

Anthus trivialis

Summer visitors normally with us from April to September, Tree Pipits are common in most parts of Great Britain, but rare in Ireland. They are not usually seen in mountain or treeless moorland areas, nor do they favour densely wooded country, but they frequent copses, orchards, the fringes of woods, and moderately timbered hills, parks and heath-land. Their preference for trees helps to distinguish them from Meadow Pipits, which usually fly up from the ground to sing, whereas Tree Pipits will rise from a tree or bush.

Despite their haunts, Tree Pipits always nest on the ground, though usually not far from a tree, whence the male will often fly up to sing. They build in a slight natural depression which they may enlarge, well hidden among long grass, bracken or other vegetation. The nest itself consists of dried grass with the addition of a little moss, and the cup is lined with finer grass and sometimes with hair.

There are from four to five eggs in a clutch, the first being laid early in May, with sometimes a second clutch following. The eggs are extremely variable in both colour and markings. The ground colour ranges in various shades from grey or cream through blue or pink to dark olive, brown or purplish-red ; the dark red, purple or brown markings vary from a few specks and blotches to dense spots and mottles, though generally the less heavy markings are found on the paler ground colours.

Tree Pipits are sometimes victimised by the Cuckoo.

Tree Pipit   *Meadow Pipit*

MEADOW PIPIT   April-July

Anthus pratensis

Meadow Pipits are fairly common and locally abundant. They haunt open and often high ground, but will come to lower areas in the winter months, and also frequent sand-dunes. They breed freely in coastal marshes and saltings.

The well-hidden nest of dried grass is built on the ground, with sometimes the addition of some moss and rootlets, and finer grass and hair lining the small neat cup.

The eggs are laid in one or two clutches with from four to six in each clutch, the first usually being laid in April. There is some variation in colour, but this is not nearly so great as in the eggs of the Tree Pipit. The ground colour is a pale cream or grey, and the close speckles, ranging from a greyish-olive to different shades of brown, vary a little in density to give a deep or slightly paler appearance.

Meadow Pipits are victimised by the Cuckoo even more frequently than their near relatives.

Rock Pipit   *Yellow Wagtail*

ROCK PIPIT   May-June

Anthus spinoletta

Rock Pipits breed only on rocky coasts, but in winter they are more widespread along coasts generally, and their numbers are probably increased by immigrants.

Holes and crevices in rocks or stone walls along the coast provide their nesting sites, and occasionally a concealed hole in a bank may be used, but the site is most usually on a cliff-face; when it is on a beach, it is often near the high-water mark. The nest is a neat structure of grass, moss and seaweed, particularly the long, narrow, grass-like varieties, and the lining is of fine grass and hair with sometimes a few feathers.

Two clutches of eggs are usually produced with four or five eggs in each, but the first is not often laid before May. There is no extreme variation in colour: the ground shade is a dirty or slightly greenish-white, and the markings consist of close speckles of greyish- or reddish-brown with, very occasionally, a denser band towards the larger end.

47

MOTACILLIDAE

YELLOW WAGTAIL   April–June
Motacilla flava

Yellow Wagtails are summer visitors, breeding
freely but locally in England, mainly in eastern,
midland and southern counties. They do not nest
in Scotland or Ireland. They are usually seen in
fairly open country, over commons, fields and
marshy land.

They nest on or near the ground, usually in a
meadow or a field of grain, but fields of other crops,
such as potatoes, are sometimes chosen, whilst
occasionally a hollow in a bank or at the foot of a
fence will be used, or a hole low in a wall or a haystack. Whatever the site, the nest is usually well
hidden and sheltered by the surrounding grass or
other plants, or by a large stone or clod of earth.
It is built of grass, moss and any other suitable and
available material, and is lined with fine rootlets and
grass, with fur, hair and feathers sometimes added.

The eggs are laid in clutches of from four to six
each, with two clutches in the year, the first in late
April or May. The eggs of many of the wagtail
family are very much alike, and it is not always easy
to distinguish one from the other. The ground
colour of these eggs is a creamy or dirty white,
densely marked with very close speckles of greyish-,
olive- or reddish-brown.

PIED WAGTAIL   April–June
Motacilla alba

Fairly widely distributed, these are probably the
best known of the wagtails.

They choose a varied selection of nesting sites : a common one is a hole in a bank or wall near a stream, others include a hollow among some rocks or outstanding tree roots, a crevice in a wood-pile or building, and even a depression under a clod of earth in open ground ; very rarely the old nest of another species will be used. The nest is built of leaves, moss, grass, roots and twigs securely felted together and lined with wool, hair and usually a few feathers.

Two or sometimes three clutches, of four to six eggs each, are laid, the first usually in April. They are a bluish- or dirty white, with tiny specks of grey, grey-black or grey-brown.

Pied Wagtails are common victims of the Cuckoo.

GREY WAGTAIL   April-June

Motacilla cinerea

Not so common as their Pied relatives, Grey Wagtails are most frequently found in hilly northern areas of the British Isles as both residents and summer visitors, but they breed locally throughout Britain, mainly in districts with fast-flowing and rocky streams.

Their nesting site is usually near a stream, the nest being built in a hollow in a bank, a wall or among rocks ; it consists of grass, leaves, moss and roots, lined with hair and sometimes a few feathers.

The first eggs are laid in April or May, often followed by a second clutch, with four to six eggs in each. They usually resemble closely those of the Yellow Wagtail, but sometimes bear one or two hair-lines towards the larger end.

Pied Wagtail

Grey Wagtail

Tree Creeper

CERTHIIDAE

TREE CREEPER   April-June

Certhia familiaris

Widely distributed and fairly common, Tree Creepers are never abundant. They frequent woods, often coniferous, parks, orchards, etc

They build behind loose bark, in a crevice in a tree trunk, and sometimes in a hole in a wall, especially one covered with some creeper. If there is room, a platform of twigs supports the nest, but otherwise this is built rather haphazardly of bark-fibres, grass, rootlets, moss and wool, with a lining of wool, softer bark-fibres and feathers.

The first clutch, containing five, six or more eggs, is laid in late April or early May, and there is often a second. The ground colour is white, with reddish-brown spots usually mainly clustered at or near the larger end.

Nuthatch

Great Tit

SITTIDAE

NUTHATCH   April-June

Sitta europaea

Nuthatches are common and widely distributed in England and Wales, except in the extreme north. They do not nest in Scotland or Ireland. Their haunts are wooded country, parks, orchards and gardens.

Holes, usually in trees but occasionally in a wall, provide nesting sites for Nuthatches. They themselves never excavate but adapt existing holes, narrowing those too large with a rim of mud or clay mixed with saliva, any cracks which appear during building being repaired at once. The nest consists of little more than a lining of bark-fibres, grass, rootlets, dead leaves and woodchips.

There is usually only one clutch of eggs in the year, laid in late April or early May and containing from five to eight or even more. The ground colour is white, sometimes faintly tinged with a pale pinkish-brown, and marked with specks and bolder spots of tan or reddish-brown ; these markings, though distinct, are seldom heavy.

51

GREAT TIT

April-June

Parus major

Great Tits are the largest of their family, and are common residents. They are widely distributed throughout the British Isles, but rare in the extreme north of Scotland and in some Scottish islands. Their haunts are many, and they are often to be seen in parks, gardens and orchards. Like Blue Tits, they are frequent visitors to the garden where fat, nuts and bones are hung up for their enjoyment.

They have almost as varied a taste in nesting sites as their relatives the Blue Tits. Their holes are usually found in a tree, a bank or wall, or among some rocks, but often more odd sites are chosen, such as an upturned flowerpot, an old can or bucket, or even a letter-box. When the hole is large the birds will collect an incredible amount of material—usually leaves, grass, moss and feathers—to provide a base for the nest, which is a felted structure of grass, wool and moss surrounding a deep cup lined with hair, fur and feathers. When the hole is smaller, a much skimpier nest is built, although there is still a deep cup.

The number of eggs in each of the two clutches is very variable, and ranges from six or seven to twelve or even fifteen ; the size of a clutch is known to depend in some way on the amount of food available, but exactly how is not yet clear. Laying begins in April or May. The ground colour of the eggs is a creamy white, marked with tan or brown spots which vary both in size and in density.

PARIDAE

BLUE TIT

April-June

Parus caeruleus

Abundant and popular, Blue Tits have a widespread distribution throughout Great Britain, but are rare or absent in some districts in the most northerly parts of Scotland and in some Scottish islands. They are to be seen almost anywhere except in closely built-up areas, and their acrobatic and perky movements are familiar to most people. They are readily attracted to gardens by bones, nuts, fat, etc., strung up as delicacies.

Blue Tits are well known for their habit of nesting in odd places, for they will choose almost any hole or cavity and will often return to the same site year after year. Holes in trees, walls and banks provide the more usual sites, but such odd places as a letter-box, an old watering can and even a lamp-post have been selected. Old nests of other birds are also used occasionally as a base for the nest. This consists of grass, hair and moss felted together, and the lining of the cup is provided by hair, fur and feathers. Like Great Tits, these birds will carry a great deal of material into the hole if it is a very large one.

There is normally only one clutch of eggs, often numbering seven or eight, but clutches of twelve and even more are not infrequently found. Laying begins in late April or early May. The eggs resemble those of other tits, the ground colour being white or creamy white and the markings consisting of tan or reddish-brown specks and spots. As with the eggs of the Great Tit, these markings vary somewhat in colour, size and density, but extremes are not very common.

53

Blue Tit

Coal Tit

COAL TIT

April-May

Parus ater

Coal Tits are not nearly so abundant as Blue Tits, though widely distributed in Great Britain and in Ireland. They have a marked preference for conifer woods.

Less varied in choice of nesting sites than either Great or Blue Tits, Coal Tits prefer natural sites such as those provided by trees—a stump often being favoured—and holes in a bank or in the ground. They will also use old nests of other birds and even a squirrel's drey. The nest is similar to those of other tits, with perhaps more feathers in the lining of the cup.

The usually single clutch contains from seven to eleven eggs and laying begins in April or early May. The eggs are larger than those of the Blue Tit, but are similar in colouring, with a white or creamy white ground shade and tan or reddish-brown markings. These consist of spots and blotches, often bolder than those on the eggs of the Blue Tit, but there is some little variation in size and in density of colour.

Marsh Tit

Willow Tit

MARSH TIT

April-June

Parus palustris

Well distributed but much less abundant than other tits, Marsh Tits do not breed in Ireland or Scotland and are only very local in some northern and western counties of England and Wales. Despite their name, they do not frequent only marshy districts, but are often found in drier haunts, especially woods and hedgerows, and are also sometimes seen in orchards and gardens.

They show a greater preference for trees as nesting sites than most of the tits, and will usually select a hole low in a rotting trunk, although occasionally they may occupy one in a bank or in the ground. The nest is built of wool, fur, hair and moss, and wood chips are occasionally used as a base, but the structure generally is slighter than the usual tit's nest.

The five to nine eggs are laid in late April or early May and sometimes a second clutch is produced. The eggs are typical of the family in colour and markings, but in some specimens the markings are clustered towards the larger end.

WILLOW TIT

April-May

Parus atricapillus

Not easily distinguished from Marsh Tits, Willow Tits are very local in distribution but do not breed north of the Scottish lowlands or in Ireland. They are sometimes found in close association with Marsh Tits.

As their name would suggest, Willow Tits prefer to make their nests in willows, though occasionally stumps of other trees, or posts, in marshy districts are chosen and, unlike Marsh Tits, these birds always excavate their own holes. The nest itself is rather slight compared with those sometimes produced by other tits, and is often little more than a cup of fur, hair and some feathers felted together and occasionally resting on wood chips. It is worth noting that, unlike others of this family, Willow Tits do not appear to favour moss in building their nests.

There is usually only one clutch of eggs, laid in late April or early May, with from six to nine eggs in the clutch. They are of the usual family type, but perhaps a little broader. The reddish-brown or buff markings consist of specks and blotches and are often profuse, rather than scattered, giving more of an all-over effect.

LONG-TAILED TIT

April-June

Aegithalos caudatus

Long-tailed Tits are well distributed except in the far north of Scotland, where they are scarce or do not breed at all. They are sociable, seldom shy and, particularly in winter, may be found in groups of a dozen or more flitting about over a hedgerow or among trees. They suffer severely in cold winters and often recover their numbers only slowly.

Their nesting site is usually in a thick bush or hedge, and it is usually between three and six feet from the ground. The nest is beautifully built in the shape of an upright oval, with a small entrance hole set a little more than half-way up. Moss, lichens, hair, wool and spiders' webs are closely woven and felted together to form a shell, and the inside is lined with hundreds of feathers—from one nest over two thousand were counted. There must be very little room left when the full clutch of eggs is laid and the hen is brooding—particularly when she is joined at night by her mate ! Both birds have to fold their long tails over their backs when in the nest.

The eggs are the smallest laid by any member of the tit family, and number from eight to twelve or even more in one clutch. Laying begins in April or May, and there is normally only one clutch. The ground colour is white or slightly creamy, marked with fine specks of a light red or reddish-brown. These markings are somewhat variable : they may be dusted all over the shell, or almost absent, or they may be confined to a broad zone near the larger end.

Long-tailed Tit *Bearded Tit*

BEARDED TIT   April-July

Panurus biarmicus

Bearded Tits are confined almost completely to one
locality, for they now breed only in East Anglia.
They frequent reed-beds and similar marshy places,
but severe winters play havoc with their numbers.
After the 1947 cold spell it is known that there were
almost certainly less than ten birds alive in Britain.

They nest in extensive reed-beds, the nest itself
resting on the ground or on a clump of dead or
rotting plants raised a few inches from the water.
The nest consists of blades of grass, sedge and reed
lined with any soft material nearby—usually reed
flowers and a few feathers.

There are two or three clutches of eggs in the
year, numbering from five to seven, sometimes more.
The first is usually laid in April.   The eggs do not
resemble those of other tits, for they are almost
equally rounded at both ends.   The ground colour
is a creamy white, marked with specks, lines and
thin streaks of liver-brown or near-black.

Red-backed Shrike   *Spotted Flycatcher*

LANIIDAE

RED-BACKED SHRIKE   May-June
Lanius collurio

Summer visitors from Africa, Red-backed Shrikes seldom arrive before May. They are very local, breeding in southern and central counties of England and Wales, but are commonest in south-east England, their haunts being waste and scrub land.

Favourite sites for the nest are dense hawthorns, thick brambles or gorse bushes. The nest, usually built about three feet up, is a bulky and rather untidy structure of twigs, roots, grass, moss and wool lined with finer roots, hair, wool and sometimes a few feathers. Birds will often breed in the same spot for several successive years.

The four to six eggs are laid in a single clutch late in May or early in June. They vary considerably, the ground colour being white, grey, greenish, yellowish-cream or salmon-pink, with spots, blotches, streaks and whirls of various shades of red, reddish-brown or grey which sometimes cover most of the shell but generally are confined to a broad zone at or near the larger end.

MUSCICAPIDAE

SPOTTED FLYCATCHER   May-July

Muscicapa striata

Spotted Flycatchers are summer visitors which arrive in May and leave in August and September. They are fairly widely distributed throughout the British Isles, although nowhere are they really common.   Their haunts are fairly general : gardens, orchards, copses and lightly wooded country.

Spotted Flycatchers use ledges, nooks or crevices for their nesting sites : they often choose a house or shed, the protection of a creeper or some trellis-work against a wall, but they are equally at home in the cleft of a branch.   Grass, hair, moss and a few rootlets, lined with soft materials, form the not very substantial nest, with sometimes the addition of spiders' webs or lichens.   Occasionally the old nest of another bird will be used, and a lining of grass, hair and feathers is all that will be added. These birds will often return to the same site year after year.

Laying begins in late May or early June, with four or five eggs in a clutch, often followed later by a second.   The eggs are rather slim and vary a little in colour.   The ground shade may be a dirty or creamy white, greyish- or bluish-green, marked with specks, spots and blotches of a slightly purplish-red or reddish-brown.   These markings vary in density and size : they may be fairly small and scattered over most of the shell or clustered towards the broader end, or they may be larger and almost merge into one another, when they often obscure most of the ground colour.

MUSCICAPIDAE

PIED FLYCATCHER   May-June

Muscicapa hypoleuca

Summer visitors from Africa, Pied Flycatchers usually arrive earlier than their close relatives. They are absent from Ireland, Scotland and most of England. Their distribution is curious, roughly embraced by a broad band extending from western Somerset northwards up to Lakeland and thence eastwards into Northumberland and Yorkshire. But the birds are extending their breeding range and, as they readily take to artificial nest-boxes, can easily be encouraged.

These birds are more particular than Spotted Flycatchers about their nesting-site : they too choose a hole or cranny, but although they do occasionally select one in a wall, they prefer to find it in a tree, often in one close to a stream or other moving water. As it is placed in a hole, the nest does not need to be very firm, and so it consists of a loosely interwoven structure of rootlets, bark-fibre, leaves, moss and hair, with a lining of hair and wool and, sometimes, a few feathers.

There is only one clutch of eggs in the year, laid in late May or early June, and there are usually five to seven eggs in the clutch, although there may occasionally be more. The eggs are generally slightly smaller than those of the Spotted Flycatcher and are not quite so slim. In colour they are completely dissimilar, for they are a uniform pale blue and bear no markings at all. It is interesting to note that although they are laid in a hole which must be fairly dark, the eggs are not white as are those of most birds laying in similar situations.

Pied Flycatcher   *Goldcrest*

REGULIDAE

GOLDCREST   April-June

Regulus regulus

Goldcrests are well distributed, although nowhere abundant. They are, however, very small—in fact, the smallest of European birds—and, with their rather inconspicuous colouring (apart from the crest), are often overlooked. They breed mostly in coniferous or mixed woods, but occasionally in more open country.

In conifer trees they usually build among the finer branches, and the nest either rests on a flattish branch—cedars are often favoured for this—or (more usually) is slung beneath one ; in both cases the overhanging twigs and leaves well conceal the nest. This is in the form of a tiny hammock or basket of skilfully interwoven moss, lichens and spiders' webs lined with hair, wool and feathers.

The eggs—seven to ten or even more—are laid in April or early May, with sometimes a second clutch following. They are small, with a creamy or brownish-white ground colour marked with tiny reddish-brown speckles, which may be scattered or dense, but which nearly always form a heavier zone at or towards the larger end.

Chiffchaff

Willow Warbler

CHIFFCHAFF

April-June

Phylloscopus collybita

Among the earliest of our summer visitors, Chiff-chaffs begin to arrive in March ; nearly all leave in September or October, but in most years a very few winter in the extreme south-west. Commonest in southern districts, they do not breed in central or north Scotland. They frequent copses and wooded park-lands with a rich undergrowth.

The nest is built amongst the undergrowth, usually about a foot above the ground. It is domed, with an entrance at the side, and is rather loosely built of grass, moss and dead leaves with a lining of finer grass, rootlets and feathers.

There are from five to seven eggs in a clutch, normally one clutch in the year, but sometimes two. The eggs are laid in late April or early May. The ground colour is a slightly glossy white, marked with specks and spots of deep purple, dark brown or a rich purplish-brown.

SYLVIIDAE

WILLOW WARBLER
May-June

Phylloscopus trochilus

Widely distributed throughout the British Isles, Willow Warblers are the most abundant of our summer visitors ; they arrive in late March or early April and leave towards the end of August or during September. They frequent bushy commons, small woods, hedgerows, orchards and gardens, and are not confined to low country, but can be seen in similar situations on hillsides.

Like Chiffchaffs, Willow Warblers build dome-shaped nests, but almost invariably the site is on the ground, with the nest often cunningly concealed by a tuft of grass or by the stems of plants. It is usually built of grass, with sometimes the addition of such materials as bracken, heather and the fine twigs and roots of other plants, also moss and dead leaves. The cup is warmly lined with plenty of feathers. The materials used and the site chosen combine to make the nest extremely difficult to find.

The normal clutch consists of five to seven eggs, and many birds are probably double-brooded in the south. The eggs are laid in May and vary little. The ground colour is usually white or a faint creamy buff, normally speckled or blotched with a light reddish-brown. These markings may be sparsely distributed over the shell or they may form a denser pattern, and they may be slightly heavier towards the larger end of the egg.

SYLVIIDAE

WOOD WARBLER

May-June

Phylloscopus sibilatrix

Wood Warblers, unlike some of their near relatives, arrive as rather late summer visitors. They reach this country late in April or early in May and have usually left by September. They are widely distributed throughout Great Britain, though they are rather local in occurrence, and are absent in Ireland and the extreme north of Scotland. As their name suggests, they frequent wooded country more exclusively than other warblers, and show a marked preference for beeches, birches and oaks.

The nest is nearly always found on the ground, usually in a ready-made hollow and well hidden by grass, bracken or other undergrowth. Dome-shaped, with a side-entrance, it is built of moss, dried grass and leaves, sometimes with the addition of some bracken. The lining of the cup is very rarely provided by feathers as in the case of the nests of Chiffchaffs and Willow Warblers, but consists of hair and fine grass.

There is only one clutch of eggs in the year, laid in late May or early June, and numbering from five to seven. The eggs are larger than those of the Willow Warbler, and have a white ground colour. The markings consist of spots and blotches of a dark shade, ranging from purplish-red through a deep reddish-brown to near-black. They are usually very profuse, and sometimes form a deep zone at or towards the larger end.

SYLVIIDAE

Wood Warbler   *Grasshopper Warbler*

GRASSHOPPER WARBLER   May-July

Locustella naevia

Arriving from the middle of April onwards, and leaving from the end of August, Grasshopper Warblers are summer visitors to the British Isles, except to central and northern districts of Scotland. They are shy and retiring birds and therefore not very often seen. They are very local in distribution and numbers may vary greatly between one season and another. Their haunts are usually marshes, but they occur on common and other waste land and are sometimes seen over high moorland, but seldom far from water of some kind.

The nesting site is generally close to the ground among grass, waterside plants, bushes or heather, and is very difficult to find as it is well hidden. The nest itself consists of dried grass or sedge with the addition of some moss or dead leaves, and has a lining of finer dried grass and perhaps some hair.

There are from four to six eggs in a clutch, laid at the end of May or early in June, with occasionally a second clutch. The eggs have a creamy white ground colour, closely marked in a light reddish-brown with fine speckles or spots which sometimes form a dense zone at or towards the larger end.

Reed Warbler   *Marsh Warbler*

REED WARBLER   May-July

Acrocephalus scirpaceus

Reed Warblers are summer visitors from late April to late September, found chiefly south of a line joining the Humber to the Mersey. They are absent from North Wales, Scotland and Ireland. Reed-beds and reed-grown dikes are their usual haunts.

The nest is usually built among reeds, but also very occasionally in growing corn, in osiers and willows. It is a wonderful structure, generally built between several stems which pass through the nest, with strips of reed or sedge interwoven with grass, moss, wool and reed-flowers, whilst the deep cup is lined with finer grass, hair and more reed-flowers ; sometimes, however, the nest is much slighter in construction.

Laying begins in mid-May in the south, with four or five eggs in a clutch and often two clutches in the year. The ground colour is a pale greenish-white with greenish, olive or grey specks, spots and blotches which usually form a dense mottling over the whole shell.

Reed Warblers are frequently victimised by the Cuckoo.

MARSH WARBLER

June-July

Acrocephalus palustris

Among our rarest birds, Marsh Warblers are late summer visitors, arriving towards the end of May or early in June and leaving during August. They breed in osier-beds and are virtually confined to Dorset, Somerset, Gloucestershire and Worcestershire. Their song is one of the finest sung by any British bird : otherwise they are almost indistinguishable in the field from the much commoner Reed Warbler.

The nest is shallow and is slung between the stems of plants such as nettles, meadow-sweet and willowherb, rather like a hammock, for the stems do not as a rule pass through the nest. This is usually a rather flimsy structure of loosely woven grass, moss and leaves, with a slight lining of hair and fine rootlets, but occasionally a nest closely resembles the bulkier, neater nest of the Reed Warbler.

The eggs are laid in a single clutch usually in June or early in July, but rarely in the last week of May, and there are four or five eggs in the clutch. They are generally easy to distinguish from those of the Reed Warbler, for they are less densely marked, with a ground colour of a dirty white often faintly tinged with a very pale lilac-blue or green. The markings range in colour from grey and olive through violet and purple to near-black, and consist chiefly of bold spots, streaks and blotches, usually clustered towards the larger end, with a powdering of finer speckles elsewhere on the shell.

SEDGE WARBLER

May-July

Acrocephalus schoenobaenus

Sedge Warblers are the most common of those warblers which frequent marshy places. Like the others, they are summer visitors, arriving in this country from the middle of April and beginning to leave again during August. They are widely distributed throughout the British Isles. Any stretch of water will attract them, from a small pond or ditch to a broad lake or wide expanse of marsh, but their haunts are usually where the surrounding vegetation grows thickly.

The nest is usually built among sedges, rushes, reeds or coarse grasses usually within a few inches of the ground. Unlike the nests of the Marsh and Reed Warblers, that of Sedge Warblers is seldom suspended between plant-stems, but is usually supported from beneath. It is neater than that of the Marsh Warbler, but not so skilfully woven as the Reed Warbler's ; it is built of grass, plant-stems and moss with a lining of grass, willow-down, hair or dead reed-heads.

There are four or five eggs in a clutch and often two clutches in the year, with laying usually beginning in May ; eggs of second clutches may rarely be found as late as the first week in August. The eggs are rather dull, usually a uniform buff or olive-yellow, sometimes with speckles and hair streaks of a darker shade.

Sedge Warbler   *Garden Warbler*

GARDEN WARBLER   May-June

Sylvia borin

Summer visitors which arrive in late April or May and leave in September, Garden Warblers, are fairly common, especially in the south, but do not breed north of mid-Scotland. Despite their name, the birds seldom frequent gardens, their usual haunts being thickets and copses where the undergrowth is dense.

A low bush or shrub, or a clump of herbage generally provides the nesting-site, for the nest itself is rarely at any height from the ground. It is rather a slight and flimsily built structure of grass and rootlets lined with hair and fine grass.

The eggs are laid in a single clutch of four or five late in May or early in June. The ground colour is whitish, tinged faintly with cream or a yellowish-green, and bears markings of various shades of brown, grey or olive-green. These consist of spots, streaks and blotches, sometimes with one or two fine lines as well, and are rather scattered over the shell. Second clutches of eggs may be commoner than is at present supposed.

Blackcap

Dartford Warbler

BLACKCAP   May-June

Sylvia atricapilla

Well distributed and fairly common except in northern Scotland, Blackcaps are summer visitors arriving in March and April and leaving in September or October.   Occasionally, however, birds may winter here, usually in the south-west.   Like Garden Warblers, Blackcaps frequent wooded situations, though generally more open ones.

The nest is built in undergrowth, thick bushes or hedges, sometimes in an evergreen, and though it is usually placed a little higher than that of the Garden Warbler, this is not always the case.   The roughly built but firm nest consists of grass, rootlets and strips of sedge interwoven and lined with hair and fine grass.

Laying begins in mid-May : there are four or five eggs in a clutch, and second clutches may not be uncommon.   There is some degree of variation in the colouring of the eggs : the ground colour is a yellowish-white or reddish tint suffused or mottled with a darker shade.   The markings consist of a few scattered spots, blotches and scribbles of dark brown.

SYLVIIDAE

DARTFORD WARBLER   April-July

Sylvia undata

The only British resident members of their family,
Dartford Warblers are now very rare, being confined
to a few counties in southern and south-western
England. They breed on commons where heather
and furze bushes are abundant.

In these plants, and particularly in heather, the
nest is built and is usually very well concealed. It is
a firm, compact structure of shoots and rootlets of
heather and furze interwoven with grass, feathers
and wool, whilst its crevices are often stopped with
moss and fragments of spiders' webs ; the cup is
lined with hair, fur and fine grass.

The eggs are laid in clutches of from four to six in
number, and there are usually two clutches in the
year, the first being laid in April and the second in
June or even early in July. The ground colour of
the eggs is a pale yellowish- or greenish-white, and
the usually profuse markings vary in shade from grey
through olive-green to a reddish-brown.

These beautiful and rare warblers have suffered
from the unworthy attentions of egg-collectors.
But they are also severely affected by cold winters
and by heath-fires in the breeding season.

SYLVIIDAE

WHITETHROAT

May-July

Sylvia communis

Whitethroats, sometimes called Greater or Common Whitethroats, are summer visitors arriving in late April and May and leaving in August and September. They are common and are widely distributed throughout the British Isles except in the extreme north of Scotland.

The nesting site is in an overgrown ditch, tangled roadside herbage, a bramble waste or a small thicket. The nest itself is built usually within a foot or two of the ground and well hidden amongst a tangle of weeds—clumps of nettles and bramble bushes are particularly favoured. The nest itself is rather loosely woven of rootlets and plant-fibres or grass, whilst the usually deep cup is lined with hair, wool and fine grass.

There are from four to six eggs in the clutch and laying begins in late May or early June, with a second clutch often following. The eggs show some degree of variation both in colour and in marking: the ground colour may be off-white or white suffused with a greenish or yellowish tinge, or sometimes it may deepen to near-brown. The markings range in colour from grey through slate-blue and olive to brown or reddish-brown, and vary considerably in form and density, for in some clutches they are scattered in rather sparse spots and blotches, whilst in others they consist of a mottling of smaller and closer speckles and streaks.

73

SYLVIIDAE

Whitethroat   *Lesser Whitethroat*

LESSER WHITETHROAT   May-June

Sylvia curruca

Not so common as Whitethroats, Lesser White-throats are more local in distribution. They do not breed in Scotland or Ireland. Their haunts are somewhat similar to those of Whitethroats, though they show more of a preference for bushes and trees.

The nest, usually placed some distance up in a tall bush or tree, is smaller and more frail than the commoner bird's, and is built of dried grass, stems and rootlets, lined with plant-fibres or, occasionally, with hair.

The eggs are laid in May or June, usually in a single clutch of from four to six. The ground colour is white, creamy or buff and the markings consist of specks and spots of lavender-grey overlaid and interspersed with spots and blotches of yellowish-, olive- or dark brown, and they are sometimes grouped into a definite zone.

Mistle Thrush   *Song Thrush*

MISTLE THRUSH   February-May

Turdus viscivorus

Storm-cocks or Mistle Thrushes are common residents, widely distributed throughout the British
Isles. They frequent copses, orchards, gardens and
tree-clad country generally and, in the winter, more
open country also.

The nesting site is variable, most usually in the
fork or on the branch of a tall tree, but also quite low
in a tree or bush, in a crevice or on the ledge of a
wall, a quarry or a cliff, even on the ground. The
nest itself, rather bulky and conspicuous, is built of
twigs, roots, grass, moss and wool, cemented on the
inside with mud over which is a lining of soft dried
grass.

There are normally two clutches of four or five
eggs, the first sometimes laid as early as February,
but more often in March. The ground colour is a
pale greenish-blue or cream tinged with a light
reddish-brown, with specks, spots and blotches
of a richer reddish-brown and of lavender-grey.

TURDIDAE

SONG THRUSH

February-July

Turdus ericetorum

Song Thrushes are even more familiar and common than their close relatives, and are widely distributed throughout the British Isles. They do not favour hilly districts, but otherwise their haunts are general, though they show a preference for trees or bushy undergrowth, parks and large gardens, even in suburban areas.

Their choice of nesting sites is more general than that of Mistle Thrushes. They will choose the fork of a tree or stout bush, a hedge, the shelter of an evergreen, a ledge or crevice in a wall or building. Twigs, roots, stems, grass, leaves, wool, paper and moss may all go into the building of the nest which, like that of the Mistle Thrush, is cemented and rounded into a saucer on the inside with mud, often mixed with plant-fibres.

The first eggs are occasionally laid in February, but March or even April is the more usual date. There are often three clutches in the year, with four or five eggs in each clutch. The ground colour is a beautifully clear pale greenish-blue—almost turquoise—and the markings consist of specks, spots and blotches of a very deep olive-green, black or reddish-brown. There is some variation in the density of these markings, but they are usually rather sparsely scattered over the shell, and very occasionally are clustered towards the larger end.

TURDIDAE

RING OUZEL   April-June

Turdus torquatus

Summer visitors to the British Isles, Ring Ouzels begin to arrive in March and most leave in September. They are widely but very locally distributed and are generally found only in moorland and mountainous country with swift-flowing streams.

The nest is often well-hidden, being built among thick clumps of heather or bracken, in crevices among rocks or under an overhanging tussock in the bank of a stream, but occasionally it is placed in an open situation on a stone ledge or in a hole in a wall or bank. The nest is similar in size and shape to that of the Blackbird, with the same mud-built cup inside lined with fine dry grass, but the outer shell is usually woven of heather and bracken stems, grass, wool and moss. Some birds build this outer shell solely of wiry grass, but, unlike Blackbirds, they do not weave in the ends of the stalks but leave them sticking out stiffly at all angles.

There are usually two clutches in the year with four eggs in each clutch, though sometimes five or six may be found ; laying begins late in April or early in May. The eggs, similar to those of the Blackbird, have a pale greenish-blue ground colour smeared and blotched with greyish- and reddish-brown. These markings are bolder than those on the eggs of the Blackbird, but generally leave more of the ground colour visible.

Ring Ousel   *Blackbird*

BLACKBIRD   March-June

Turdus merula

Blackbirds are abundant and common almost every-where, being widely distributed throughout the British Isles. They are well known in the parks and gardens of the towns, and in the country frequent hedgerows, copses, orchards and wooded land. They are, however, rarely seen on really high ground, where they are usually replaced by Ring Ouzels.

Trees, bushes and hedges and, occasionally, a ledge or hole in a wall or building, provide sites for the nest, which is usually built a few feet up, but may sometimes be placed on the ground. It is a fairly large but neat structure of interwoven grass, twigs and rootlets, cemented on the inside with mud which forms a smooth cup and is covered with a lining of dry grass.

The eggs are laid in two or three clutches of from four to six each, the first normally appearing in March. The ground colour of pale greenish-blue is usually marked with close, fine speckles of tan or reddish-brown, sometimes forming a heavier zone at the larger end.

TURDIDAE

Wheatear

Whinchat

WHEATEAR

April–June

Oenanthe oenanthe

Early summer visitors, Wheatears begin to arrive in March and leave again in September and October. They are widely distributed in favourable districts throughout the British Isles, and they frequent moorlands, mountains and hillsides, sand dunes and waste and rough land generally.

The nesting site varies with the locality : on high ground and in rocky areas, the birds will choose a hole in a wall or rock, or a hollow in the ground sheltered by a boulder, a cluster of rocks or a clod of earth ; on lower slopes and among sand dunes, a rabbit burrow or other excavated tunnel will serve. The nest itself is a loosely woven structure of grass, roots, stems and moss lined with such soft materials as dry grass, hair, fur, wool and feathers.

There are five or six eggs—rarely more—in a clutch and normally only one clutch in the year, laid in late April or in early May. The eggs are a very pale and slightly greenish-blue, usually bearing no markings at all, but very occasionally there may be a few small spots of reddish-brown.

TURDIDAE

WHINCHAT May-June

Saxicola rubetra

Whinchats are rather late summer visitors, for they arrive during the latter part of April and the beginning of May, leaving again in late August and during September, although a few may linger until October. Whinchats are widely distributed throughout the British Isles, but are local in occurrence, and are absent from parts of Ireland. Their haunts are commons, fields, marshes, heaths and waste and open land generally.

The nest is usually built on or close to the ground, and is very difficult to find, being well hidden, partly by the nature of its site and partly by virtue of the materials used in its construction. Typical sites are clumps of rough grass, a low bush—usually furze—and a hollow in the ground concealed by the surrounding plants or by a clod of earth. The nest consists of dry grass and moss, and its cup is lined with finer grass and hair.

There is normally only a single clutch of eggs, but a second is occasionally found. The clutch contains from four to six eggs, seldom more, and is laid towards the end of May or at the beginning of June. The eggs are often rounded rather than sharply pointed at the smaller end, and have a fairly deep greenish-blue ground colour. Many specimens bear no markings at all, but some are faintly and sparsely spotted with reddish-brown : when these markings are present they are usually found chiefly towards the larger end.

STONECHAT

April-June

Saxicola torquata

Although Stonechats are largely resident in the British Isles, there is a dispersal from the breeding grounds in winter. Like their close relatives, the Whinchats, these birds have a fairly wide distribution but are somewhat local. Stonechats frequent country similar to that favoured by Whinchats, but prefer a little more cover, particularly that provided by furze and brambles ; they are often most common near southern and western coasts.

The nesting sites as well are similar to those of the related bird, and are close to or on the ground and very well concealed. The nest is placed in or beneath a clump of grass, furze, bramble or heather and is built of grass, small twigs and roots, moss and occasionally fur or wool, whilst the lining consists of fine grass, hair and often a few feathers.

Laying begins as a rule in April and the eggs are laid in clutches of from four to six in number, with normally two clutches in the year. The eggs are slightly more elongated than those of the Whinchat, the smaller end being more pointed. The ground colour is paler and has slightly more of a greenish tinge to the blue ; it is powdered with very fine reddish-brown speckles which often form a heavier zone at or towards the larger end.

Stonechat   *Redstart*

REDSTART   May-June

Phoenicurus phoenicurus

Redstarts are summer visitors which arrive in April
and May and leave in September and October.
They are widely distributed but local, scarce in the
extreme west and absent from Ireland. In general
they frequent wooded land, particularly where the
trees are old, and they are also seen around quarries
and ruins and in rocky country.

These birds use a wide selection of nesting sites—
cracks, holes and crevices in old or rotting trees and
stumps, and in rocks, ruins and quarries, are perhaps
the most common, but old Woodpecker cavities and
holes in the ground—and in occupied houses—have
also been used. The nest, however, is always well
hidden, and is rather loosely woven of grass, rootlets,
bark-fibre, moss and wool, with a lining of feathers
and hair.

The eggs are laid in May or June in a clutch of
five, six, or even more. They are a uniform clear
and slightly greenish-blue and only very infrequently
do they bear sparse flecks of a pale reddish-brown.

Black Redstart   *Nightingale*

BLACK REDSTART   April-June

Phoenicurus ochrurus

Formerly known in this country chiefly as local migrants and winter visitors, Black Redstarts have in recent years taken to nesting here more regularly, though in very small numbers. They are mainly confined in the breeding season to London and the Home Counties.

The nesting sites are mainly in ruined buildings, and the bombed areas of London have afforded them some excellent sites. The nest is built in cracks, pipes and crannies in walls and buildings or among rocks. Plant-stems, grass and moss are woven into a rather loose structure, which is then lined with hair and feathers.

There are from four to six eggs in a clutch, and often two clutches in the year, possibly more, with the first being laid in April. The eggs are generally a little larger and rounder than those of the Redstart, and are usually a rather glossy white, occasionally suffused lightly with pale blue.

NIGHTINGALE   May

Luscinia megarhyncha

Nightingales are summer visitors, arriving from the middle of April onwards and leaving this country again in late August and September. Commonest in the south, East Anglia and the east Midlands, they seldom breed north of Lincolnshire and Staffordshire and are absent from Wales and Cornwall. They are shy and retiring birds, and frequent thickets, shrubby copses and coppices.

In such situations the nest is built, either on the ground or close to it among the roots or lower shoots of a bush or hedge, at the base of a tree or in a clump of grass or other plants. It consists of a rather bulky mass of dead leaves, often mainly from oaks, which the birds gather up and form into an untidy shape with grass. The cup is lined with finer grass and some more leaves, with the occasional addition of some hair. The site in thick, overgrown cover, the general untidiness of the structure and the use of local material all help to make the nest extremely difficult to find, for it blends perfectly with its surroundings.

The single clutch of eggs is laid in May, towards the beginning of the month as a rule, and consists of from four to six in number. The ground colour of the eggs is a rich olive-green—sometimes almost olive-blue—or a deep olive-brown. There are no markings, and the shell is usually evenly coloured, but occasionally it may have a mottled appearance.

ROBIN

March-June

Erithacus rubecula

Most popular of British birds, Robins are widely distributed and generally common throughout the British Isles. Familiar and friendly in our gardens, even in towns, Robins also frequent thick hedges and bushes and the tangled undergrowth of copses and woods.

The nesting site is almost anywhere or anything that can offer a hole, depression or other cavity, for these birds have a wide taste which sometimes borders on the eccentric. A hole in a sheltered bank, ditch or wall, a crevice in a tree or amongst a creeper, are some of the natural sites chosen, but sometimes an old watering-can, flower-pot, kettle, hat or other rejected article will be used. Among some of the odder places in which nests have been built are the pulpit of a church, the cubby-hole in the cabin of a lorry, the bristles of an upturned broom, the handle-bars of a bicycle stored in a shed, a piece of machinery in a busy factory and a railway truck in use. The nest itself is a rather bulky structure of grass, moss and dead leaves softly lined with fine grass, hair and a few feathers.

The eggs are laid in clutches of five or six, with two or three clutches in the year, the first often being laid in March. The ground colour of the eggs is white or creamy buff, marked with light reddish-brown. The markings vary from fine speckles to bold blotches or mottles, and from a few scattered spots, sometimes clustered towards the larger end, to a great many covering the whole of the shell.

Robin

Hedge Sparrow

PRUNELLIDAE

HEDGE SPARROW   March-July

Prunella modularis

Hedge Sparrows are not sparrows at all, and are often known by their other name of Dunnocks. They are widely distributed throughout the British Isles. Their haunts are copses, hedges, shrubberies, gardens and moorlands, and they are quite common, though often overlooked because of their quiet habits and inconspicuous plumage.

A bank, hedge, bush or evergreen are among the sites chosen for the nest. The nest is usually supported by a small platform of twigs and is neatly built of finer twigs, rootlets, grass and moss, lined with hair, moss and wool.

There are four or five eggs in a clutch and two or three clutches in the year, the first being laid in March or April. The colour is a uniform and beautiful greenish-blue, and the eggs are not unlike those of the Redstart.

In the south the Cuckoo will often lay in a Hedge Sparrow's nest.

Swallow

Wren

HIRUNDINIDAE

SWALLOW   May-August

Hirundo rustica

Widely distributed summer visitors from April to October, Swallows are generally confined to low ground.

The nest, a shallow saucer of mud lined with grass and feathers, is usually built on a beam in barns, stables and outhouses, and may be used for several years in succession.

Two, three or even four clutches of from four to six eggs are laid. The ground colour is white, lightly spotted all over with reddish-brown or various shades of grey through to black.

TROGLODYTIDAE

WREN   April-June

Troglodytes troglodyteş

Wrens are widely distributed and fairly common.

Any hole, fork or crevice shelters the nest, which is extremely neat, domed, with a side entrance, and usually consists of any handy material—grass, leaves, moss, etc., lined with hair, moss or feathers.

Two clutches of from five to eight (sometimes more) eggs are laid ; they are white and usually lightly spotted with reddish-brown.

Dipper   *Kingfisher*

CINCLIDAE

DIPPER   April-July

Cinclus cinclus

Widely but locally distributed except east of a
line drawn from the Wash to The Exe estuary,
Dippers haunt fast-moving rivers and streams.

The nesting site is near water, in a bank, under
a wooden bridge or among rocks, and the large,
domed nest has a side entrance and is built of moss
or dry leaves and grass and similarly lined.

The white eggs are laid in two or three clutches
with from four to six eggs in each.

ALCEDINIDAE

KINGFISHER   April-July

Alcedo atthis

Kingfishers, though not common, are widely distributed except in northern Scotland, where they do
not nest. Their main haunts are slower-moving
waters and lakes.

A tunnel two or three feet long in a bank (usually
overhanging water) leads slightly upwards to the
nesting hole, where fish-bones and disgorged pellets
provide a platform for the eggs.

Two clutches with from six to eight in each are
usual, the eggs being rather round, and glossy white.

House Martin   *Sand Martin*

HOUSE MARTIN   May-September
Delichon urbica

Widely distributed summer visitors from April to October, House Martins are quite common, though very local in parts of Scotland and Ireland.

The nest is usually built against a vertical wall below eaves, but occasionally in a building. Nests are also sometimes built on overhanging cliffs, both coastal and inland. The nest is made of mud with a small hole near the top.

Two or sometimes three clutches of white eggs are laid, four or five in each clutch. It is not unusual to find young birds still in the nest in early October.

SAND MARTIN   May-July
Riparia riparia

Also summer visitors, but more local in distribution, Sand Martins may be seen from March to September around water, gravel-pits, cliffs and sandy banks.

The birds nest in colonies, each pair excavating an upward-sloping tunnel, usually about two or three feet long, the end of which is lined with straw, grass, feathers and, near the coast, with seaweed.

Two clutches of four or five white and rather narrow eggs are laid.

NIGHTJAR

May-July

Caprimulgus europaeus

Nightjars, sometimes called Night-hawks or Goatsuckers, are rather late summer visitors, seldom arriving before the beginning of May and leaving again towards the end of August and early in September. They are widely but locally distributed throughout the British Isles ; seldom seen on the wing during the day unless flushed, they are crepuscular birds, feeding largely on moths and other nocturnal insects. Their haunts are moorlands, commons and wooded and waste land generally, particularly that covered by heather, bracken, etc.

The nesting site is on the ground in such situations, especially where a litter of broken twigs and branches, fragments of bark or a tangle of bracken breaks up the ground surface. For no nest is built, and the sole protection for the eggs is the way in which their own colouring and that of the sitting bird merge with their surroundings.

There are only two eggs in a clutch, with two clutches in the year, the first usually being laid at the end of May. The eggs are equally rounded at both ends and have a dirty or creamy white ground colour. The markings consist of spots and blotches of brown or various shades from grey through purple to near-black superimposed on blotches and patches of a pale, sometimes lavender-tinged, grey.

Swift

*Green
Woodpecker*

APODIDAE

SWIFT   May-June

Apus apus

Familiar summer visitors, most Swifts arrive early
in May and leave in August. They are widely distributed throughout the British Isles, except in the
extreme north. They are sociable birds, and may
be seen in small groups wheeling and twisting over-
head almost anywhere, even in towns.

The nest is built in a hole or crevice in a wall or
building (a favourite site being in neglected thatch),
in a cliff or tree, under the rafters of roofs or in
church towers. A few pieces of straw, grass, moss,
feathers or similar litter are glued together with the
birds' saliva to form the shallow, saucer-like nest.

The eggs are laid in a single clutch of two or three
at the end of May or the beginning of June. They
are rather long and narrow, and have a dull white or
occasionally creamy ground colour with no markings.

GREEN WOODPECKER

April-May

Picus viridis

Green Woodpeckers, called Yaffles in some parts, are fairly well distributed in England and Wales, but do not normally breed in Scotland or Ireland. They seldom frequent dense woodlands, but seem to prefer more sparsely wooded areas, such as parks, copses, commons and gardens, particularly where the trees are old.

The nesting site is a hole in a dead or rotting tree at a height which varies considerably—at times it may be a few feet up, at others, twenty or thirty feet above the ground. A hole about three inches in diameter is first bored horizontally into the tree to a depth of a few inches, and then for about a foot a shaft is dropped perpendicularly, at the bottom of which a small space is hollowed out for the nest. This consists simply of a small pile of soft wood chips.

There is only one clutch of eggs, varying in number from four to seven, and usually laid in late April or in May. The eggs are usually elliptical— that is, rounded more or less equally at both ends— and are a glossy white that may, however, become discoloured in a damp nest.

LESSER SPOTTED WOODPECKER May-June

Dryobates minor

The smallest of the family, Lesser Spotted or Barred Woodpeckers breed only in England as far north as Yorkshire and Cheshire and in some eastern counties of Wales. Generally rather uncommon, they are small and retiring in habit.

*Lesser Spotted
Woodpecker*

Great Spotted Woodpecker

The nesting hole is usually bored in a rotten branch, the site varying from a few to sixty feet above the ground, and measures only about an inch and a half across, while the shaft may be more than a foot deep.

The single clutch of from four to eight glossy white eggs is laid in late May or early June.

GREAT SPOTTED WOODPECKER May-June

Dryobates major

Great Spotted or Pied Woodpeckers are not uncommon in England and Wales and in lowland Scotland and are spreading northwards through the Highlands. They are not found in Ireland. Woods and parkland, particularly with old timber, are favoured haunts.

The usual woodpecker hole is excavated at least twelve feet up : its entrance is between two and three inches in diameter.

Four to seven creamy white and glossy eggs are laid in a single clutch, usually towards the end of May.

WRYNECK

May

Jynx torquilla

Unlike other members of the wood-pecker family, Wrynecks are not resident in the British Isles, but are summer visitors. They arrive towards the end of March or in the first weeks of April and leave again during September. They are mainly confined now to a few midland, eastern and south-eastern counties, being rare in all other areas and apparently diminishing in numbers. Their haunts are similar to those of other woodpeckers, but they occasionally also frequent hedges and wooded lanes.

The nesting site is in a hole or crevice, but, unlike most woodpeckers, Wrynecks will rarely, if ever, excavate their own holes, but will make use of an existing one. Trees, banks and even walls or buildings may provide a suitable cavity, and the birds often return to the same site year after year. They do not build a nest, but if there is any litter which has drifted into or been left in the hole, then the birds will not clear it out, but leave it as a lining.

There is usually only one clutch of eggs in the year, containing from six to ten (sometimes even more) eggs, and laying, though it may occasionally be a little earlier, normally begins in May. The eggs are a glossy white, about the same size as those of the Lesser Spotted Woodpecker, but generally slightly broader.

CUCKOO   May-June

Cuculus canorus

Cuckoos are summer visitors, arriving from the second week in April onwards and leaving again in July and August, though birds of the year linger into September. They are widely distributed and common throughout the British Isles.

Our Cuckoos do not build nests, but deposit their eggs in the nests of other birds. It was formerly believed that they laid each egg on the ground and carried it in their bills to the chosen nest, but it is now known that they lay direct into the nest. A surprising number of different birds are chosen as foster-parents : Meadow Pipits, Hedge Sparrows, Tree Pipits, Pied Wagtails, Reed Warblers and Robins are freely used as fosterers.

Laying begins in May, and usually from ten to fifteen eggs are laid, normally every other day, one to a nest. They show a great range of colour and marking, which often results in the eggs resembling those of other birds, but an egg does not always match those of its foster-parents. The young bird ejects the other eggs or young and so secures the undivided attention of its foster-parents.

LITTLE OWL

April-May

Athene noctua

Introduced into this country from the Continent towards the end of the last century, Little Owls have now established themselves very firmly, and have spread from half a dozen counties into all parts of England and Wales and have even been recorded from Scotland. Although active after dusk, they are also more active by day than most owls, frequenting copses and wooded land generally, quarries, ruins and open country.

The nesting site is provided by a hollow or cavity in trees, rocks, walls and quarry-faces, or even in a quite unsheltered patch of open ground. No attempt is made to build a nest, but any litter, such as dead grass and leaves, that may be in the hole will be left as a lining.

There are four or five, sometimes six, eggs in a clutch and as a rule only one clutch in the year ; this is laid in April or May. The dull white eggs are somewhat broad and elliptical—that is, they are equally rounded at both ends—and this gives them a rather squat appearance.

LONG-EARED OWL

March-April

Asio otus

Long-eared Owls are widely but extremely locally distributed throughout the British Isles. On the wing during the night, they are seldom seen in the daytime, roosting in trees until dusk. They show a preference for firs and frequent woods and hillsides where those trees are found.

These birds do not build for themselves, but generally make use of the deserted nest of another bird such as a Magpie, Crow, Jay, Hawk or Wood Pigeon, or even a squirrel's drey. The old nest is often trampled down to provide a more or less flat base on which the eggs rest. Sometimes, however, even when suitable trees are available, the nesting site will be on the ground in a bramble clump or amongst a sheltered litter of dead twigs and leaves.

The eggs are laid in March or early April in a single clutch of from three to five in number. They are white and rather round, larger than those of the Little and Short-eared Owls but smaller than those of the Tawny Owl.

SHORT-EARED OWL March-June

Asio flammeus

Resident Short-eared Owls breed mainly in Scotland and the north of England, but a few pairs nest regularly in East Anglia and occasionally elsewhere. Unlike most owls, these do not frequent woods, but on the contrary appear to avoid trees, preferring the open country of fields, marshes, fens, sand-dunes, moorland and hills. They are more active by day than any other British owl.

The nesting site is always on the ground, in a hollow sheltered by surrounding plants such as grass, heather, bracken or sedge. There is no real attempt to build a nest, but the hollow may be lined with scraps of suitable material nearby or simply with the existing vegetation.

There is usually only one clutch of eggs in the year, laid sometime between late March and early June, and containing from four to eight eggs, although more have occasionally been found. The eggs are a dull white, somewhat round, and very little smaller than those of the Long-eared Owl.

TAWNY OWL   March-April

Strix aluco

Tawny Owls, also called
Wood or Brown Owls,
are widely distributed
in suitable localities
throughout Great Bri-
tain, except in the
extreme north. They
do not breed in Ire-
land. They frequent
woodlands and occa-
sionally well-wooded
parks and gardens.
They roost by day, often
in a hollow tree, and are
seldom active until dusk.

The birds prefer a hollow
tree for their nesting site, although
they will sometimes make use of other sites,
such as the deserted nest of another bird, an old
squirrel's drey, a hole in rocks, cliffs or ruins, and
even a rabbit burrow. No nesting material is used,
although the eggs may rest on any soft litter already
in the hole.

The two to four eggs of the single clutch are laid
at intervals of about forty-eight hours or more in
March or April. They are the largest of those laid by
the owl family, and are white or faintly creamy in
colour and rounded in shape.

BARN OWL   April-May

Tyto alba

Often called White or Screech Owls, Barn Owls are widely distributed throughout the British Isles except in the far north of Scotland. But in most areas they are all too scarce. In spite of the fact that they feed largely on rats and mice, these fine and useful birds are still shot by the superstitious and those ignorant of their habits. They occasionally hunt by day, especially on dull winter afternoons, but are mainly active in twilight and at night.

Like Tawny Owls, these birds will sometimes select a hollow tree or a crevice among rocks for a nesting site, but they will more frequently choose a beam or rafter in a barn or other building, or a ledge in a ruin or quarry-face. No proper nest is made, but the eggs usually rest on pellets disgorged by the parent birds.

There are from three to eight, occasionally more, eggs in a clutch and often two clutches in the year. The white eggs are very similar to those of the Long-eared Owl, but they may sometimes be a little more elongated, though still more or less equally rounded at both ends.

PEREGRINE FALCON

April-May

Falco peregrinus

Peregrine Falcons are the largest resident members of the falcon family in the British Isles, and although their numbers have been reduced by persistent harrying and killing so that they are no longer common, they are by no means rare in favourable localities. They are most common in wild and rugged coastal and mountainous districts, and are therefore found mostly in Wales, Ireland and Scotland and in a few parts of northern England. Their breeding haunts are high, inaccessible cliffs and peaks where on some vantage point they will perch ready to descend with their powerful and terrifying stoop on the other birds which form their prey.

A ledge or platform on a steep rocky cliff provides the nesting site, which in the case of falcons and related birds of prey is called the eyrie. There is no attempt to build a proper nest, but a rough hollow is found or is scraped out for the eggs. Occasionally a hollow containing a few sticks may be used, or even the deserted nest of another bird, such as the Raven or Hooded Crow.

There is usually only one clutch of eggs in the year, laid in April or early May, and although later clutches have been found, these may have been laid by birds whose first clutch had been destroyed. The clutch contains two, three, or four eggs, the ground colour of which is usually a rich orange- or reddish-

Peregrine Falcon

brown, but is occasionally a creamy or buffish-white suffused or mottled with a rich tan. The markings are variable, and consist of specks, spots, mottles, streaks and blotches of a warm dark brown which at times looks almost black.

HOBBY   May-June

Falco subbuteo

Summer visitors to Great Britain, Hobbies are the only members of the falcon family in the British

Isles which are not resident. They arrive in May and are rarely seen later than the end of September. They are nowhere abundant, but some pairs nest regularly in southern and south-eastern counties of England. Further north they become rare, and are seldom seen north or west of the Mid-lands. It is a tragedy that these beautiful little falcons should still be persistently har-ried by the gamekeeper and the egg-collector. Hobbies prefer wood-ed belts in open country rather than thick woodlands. Though feeding to a considerable extent on insects, they are extremely fast fliers and have been known to strike successfully at Swallows on the wing.

The nesting site is always in a tree, the old or deserted nests of other birds (often those of the Carrion Crow or Jay) being used.

The eggs are laid in late May or early June. There is only one clutch in the year, and it contains two, three or four eggs ; a second clutch may be laid if the first meets with some disaster. The ground colour of the eggs varies from a yellowish-buff to a reddish-tan, and the uniform markings, which usually cover the whole shell profusely, consist of specks, spots and mottlings of a deep reddish- or nigger-brown.

FALCONIDAE

MERLIN   May

Falco columbarius

Merlins are the smallest members of the British
falcons, but they make up for their lack of size in
boldness and courage. As breeding birds they
frequent higher moorland and the lower mountains,
especially where there is a good covering of heather.
They do not breed in midland, eastern or southern
England, but are winter visitors to coasts and estuaries in those parts.

As with all falcons, no nest is built, the eggs
usually being laid on the ground in a hollow amongst
heather or similar vegetation which will give some
concealment to the eggs. Somewhere near the nest
the parent birds always have a look-out post, provided by a rock, tree-stump or similar raised
vantage-point ; this may often be recognised by the
rejected remains of the birds' prey scattered around
it.

There is only one clutch of eggs in the year, unless
some accident overtakes the first, and the number
of eggs in the clutch varies from three to five.
The ground colour ranges from a creamy buff to a
reddish-tan, while the markings consist of specks,
spots, blotches and mottlings of a deep reddish- or
nigger-brown. These markings may occasionally be
heavier towards the larger end, but are more often
evenly distributed over the whole shell, usually
covering it with a close, dense mottling.

FALCONIDAE

KESTREL

Falco tinnunculus

Our commonest falcons, both in numbers and in range, Kestrels are widely distributed throughout the British Isles. They are often called "Windhovers" from their usual habit of hovering motionless over one spot for seconds on end, looking out for prey on the ground below. In the past they have often been severely persecuted as game-poachers, and in spite of the fact that we now know that mice and voles and insects are their main items of food, the old prejudice against anything with a hooked beak dies hard, so that there are districts where the birds are still uncommon. They have a wide variety of haunts—rocks and moors on high ground, woods and pastures on downland, open fields and meadows on lower ground and cliffs along the coast.

The nesting site varies with the district frequented by the birds. The most usual sites are ledges (often inside buildings) or deserted tree-nests such as those of the Carrion Crow ; rarely is the nest on the ground, except in Orkney, where ground nesting is almost habitual. Virtually no nesting material is used.

The eggs are laid towards the end of April or in May ; there is only one clutch in the year, unless some disaster overtakes it, when a second will usually be laid. There are normally four or five eggs in the clutch, but six or even more have been recorded. The ground colour is creamy, yellowish-buff or light tan, and the markings consist of specks, spots, blotches and mottlings of a rich reddish- or nigger-brown. They vary a little in density, and

Merlin   *Kestrel*

are sometimes more thickly clustered towards the
larger end, but most usually they form a dense
marbling over the whole shell.

Like the majority of birds-of-prey, Kestrels have,
in the past, been often ruthlessly destroyed.
Although they have enjoyed legal protection for
many years, some still find their way to the gibbets
of game-keepers. Yet they feed almost entirely on
small voles, mice and shrews.

GOLDEN EAGLE   March-April

Aquila chrysaëtus

Golden Eagles breed in Scotland, mainly in the
Highlands and the west. They flourish most in the
deer forests ; in spite of legal protection they are
still destroyed on grouse moors. But Scottish

landowners have done much to help to save these fine birds from the fate of the Osprey and the Sea-eagle, whilst the Royal Society for the Protection of Birds spends several hundred pounds a year on their protection. Thus encouraged, though still scarce, they are very slowly increasing in numbers and in 1953 a pair successfully bred in Ireland—the first nesting record from that country since 1910.

The nest is sometimes built in the upper branches of a tree, but is more usually placed on a high, rocky, but not necessarily inaccessible ledge ; the birds will often return to the same site, but not always the following year—it may be that each pair has two or three sites which they use in turn. The nest is a large, untidy structure of branches, sticks and heather, lined with grass, moss, ferns and sprigs of heather. When a previous site is revisited, the old nest is repaired and added to, so that eventually it becomes a bulky mass up to two feet in height, possibly six feet across at the base and with a cup a foot or more in diameter.

The single clutch of two, or very occasionally three, eggs is laid in late March or early April, and the birds will seldom replace it if it is destroyed. The ground colour of the eggs varies from white to a creamy buff, and is marked with spots, streaks and blotches of reddish-purple and reddish- or a darker brown. These markings are seldom uniform, even in one clutch, which may often have one plain and one marked egg.

ACCIPITRIDAE

COMMON BUZZARD   April–May

Buteo buteo

Common Buzzards, once very scarce, have increased in recent years and are now locally common in south-west England, Wales, the Lake District and in parts of Scotland—mainly in the west. Their slow eastward trend is retarded by thoughtless shooting. Their favourite haunts are wild craggy heights, cliffs and woodlands.

The nesting site is usually provided either by a high fork in a tree or by a deep ledge on a rocky cliff or hillside. Like that of the Golden Eagle, the nest of the Common Buzzard is a large and rather untidy structure of branches, sticks and heather stems and roots. It is lined with grass, wool, sticks, lichens, and small branches or ivy twigs.

There is only one clutch of eggs in the year, laid towards the end of April or in the first weeks of May. It usually contains either two or three eggs, although four have been recorded. They have a ground colour which ranges from a faintly greyish- or greenish-white to a creamy buff, while the markings consist of spots, streaks and blotches of reddish-olive or a darker brown, interspersed here and there with pale reddish-purple mottlings. The markings vary a little in distribution : in some specimens they are scattered more or less evenly over the whole shell, while in others they are clustered at and towards the larger end, with a few odd marks elsewhere on the shell. Clutches are seldom uniform, often containing one plain and two marked eggs, but the same bird reproduces its own pattern faithfully year after year.

ACCIPITRIDAE

Common Buzzard

Buzzards are impressive in the air, gliding round in wide circles, occasionally with a series of slow wing flaps, and sometimes rising to great heights on the up-currents. They are large birds and are sometimes mistaken for Golden Eagles, but the latter are really huge and majestic.

Considering its size, the call of the Buzzard—a rather weird, plaintive mewing—seems strangely inappropriate.

MARSH HARRIER
Circus aeruginosus

May

Now known in the British Isles chiefly as uncommon spring and autumn migrants, Marsh Harriers formerly nested in various suitable localities in Britain and Ireland. A few birds still breed in East Anglia, and occasionally elsewhere —in 1945 a pair nested in North Wales. Marsh Harriers, as their common name suggests, frequent marshes and reed-beds, particularly where the plant-growth is lush and plentiful.

The nest is usually well hidden among dense reeds or other marsh- or water-plants. It is a large and rather untidy structure of sticks, reeds, sedges and similar material, with a lining of grass and the softer parts of suitable plants in the vicinity. The base of stout sticks, reed-stems, etc., is built up to provide a platform to keep the lined cup clear of the surrounding water or soggy ground.

The eggs are laid in May, usually towards the end of the month, and there is only the one clutch in the year. It contains from three to five eggs, the ground colour of which is white suffused with a creamy, greyish or faintly bluish tinge. Usually this is unmarked, but it may occasionally bear a few scattered spots of tan or brown.

MONTAGU'S HARRIER   May

Circus pygargus

Montagu's Harriers are uncommon summer visitors to Great Britain, arriving from mid-April onwards and leaving again during October or, very occasionally, as late as November. They have been severely persecuted in the past, and thoughtless nest-raiders have lessened their numbers still further, so that at one time only a few pairs nested in this country. But they have increased and, though still rare, now breed in a number of scattered localities in England and Wales, chiefly in the south-west, and have bred in Scotland.

The nesting site is usually on the ground among heather, marsh-plants or rocks, but a low bush or some trampled plants will also serve. The nest varies somewhat in size : sometimes it is little more than a scrape in the ground with a scanty lining, but at others it is quite a large structure of sticks, twigs, heather, reeds or grass.

The single clutch of eggs is laid in late May, and contains from four to six eggs. These resemble closely those of Marsh Harriers, though they are a little smaller and are sometimes more rounded at the smaller end.

ACCIPITRIDAE

HEN HARRIER

April-May

Circus cyaneus

Although up to the end of the last century Hen Harriers nested in many districts of the British Isles, breeding birds are now found only on certain Scottish islands and (a very few) in the Scottish Highlands. Few birds have been more persistently persecuted in the alleged interests of game. Although grouse chicks are undeniably sometimes taken, the status of these birds is one of the worst blots in the sportsman's copybook.

Like the other two Harriers, these birds build on or very close to the ground. The nesting site is among tall heather, bracken or other plants, usually screened at the sides but open to the sky. The nest itself consists of sticks, heather, bracken, or any suitable material at hand. The lining of soft grass varies in quantity—in some nests it is abundant, in others, very skimpy.

There is only one clutch in the year, laid in late April or May, and containing from four to six eggs. These resemble those of the other Harriers, and, like them, may in damp situations be considerably stained with brown by rotting vegetation.

SPARROW HAWK

April-May

Accipiter nisus

Sparrow Hawks are resident and, after Kestrels, the commonest of our birds of prey, despite severe persecution. They are well distributed throughout the British Isles in wooded districts, hunting among the trees and over the surrounding open country.

The nesting site is usually high in a tree (a conifer for preference), but may on occasions be on a cliffledge. Sparrow Hawks like a ready-made base for their nests, and generally build on the old nest of another bird—often a member of the Crow family—or sometimes on a squirrel's deserted drey. The nest itself is a large, rather flat and untidy collection of sticks and twigs lined with such softer materials as down and bark-fibre.

The single clutch of eggs, from four to six in number, is laid at the end of April or during May. The ground colour of the eggs is white, sometimes tinged with blue or green, and the markings, often interspersed with purple blotches, are a rich reddish-brown. They vary considerably : generally consisting of spots and blotches, they may be clustered together at one end in a group or a solid cap, they may form a zone, or they may be scattered more generally over the shell. Quite often one egg in a clutch will be almost unmarked.

KITE

April-May

Milvus milvus

Now restricted to a few wild districts in Wales, Kites were formerly well distributed in Great Britain. Up to the beginning of the last century they were common and well-known birds of the wooded valleys, frequently visiting the streets and gardens of towns and villages, where they acted as useful and necessary scavengers. Unfortunately, to outweigh this service, they were also liable to raid grounds and farmyards for young and weakly birds, although these by no means formed the main items of their diet. Game-preservers and farmers then began so severe a persecution that by the end of the century the birds had become very scarce, the few remaining pairs having retired to remote hill districts ; nest-robbing by Carrion Crows and thoughtless egg-stealers also helped to reduce the numbers. Many years ago the Royal Society for the Protection of Birds, realising that Kites were threatened with extinction, began to organise some measures of protection for them, and there is now hope that the birds may, in time, increase ; but at present there are probably less than twelve pairs in existence.

The large nest is built well up in a tree or, very occasionally, on a rocky ledge, and consists of a flat, untidy structure of large sticks and branches. Between these is crammed all manner of litter— paper, grass, rags, wool and roots, all stuffed into the crevices among the wood. Similar materials—wool, hair, paper, string, in fact, any bits of rubbish which the birds can find—form the lining of the cup. Kites usually build their own nests completely, but occasionally they may select the old or deserted nest of another bird, adding to and adapting it according to their own requirements.

There is only one clutch of eggs in the year, laid as a rule in mid-April, though sometimes more towards the end of the month or, very infrequently, at the beginning of May. The clutch contains two or three eggs, largish in size and usually rather more rounded than pointed at the smaller end. The ground colour is either a dirty, greyish-white or a pale creamy buff, while the markings consist of specks, spots, streaks, lines and blotches of reddish- or nigger-brown. These markings are generally rather sparsely scattered over the whole shell, but may sometimes be clustered more towards one end

ARDEIDAE

HERON   February-April

Ardea cinerea

Herons are widely distributed throughout the British Isles. They are called " Cranes " in some districts, but should not be confused with real Cranes, which ceased to be resident in this country several centuries ago. Herons are generally sociable birds, and may often be seen in small groups near their haunts, which are damp woods, marshes, lakes, rivers and river-estuaries. They may sometimes be stalking through the shallows, but more often will be standing motionless on a post or jutting rock, heads sunk between their shoulders. In this seemingly dejected attitude they show little appearance of being watchful, but in fact they are ready to pounce on any hapless water creature that comes along. Fish form a main item in their diet, especially eels, and they will also eat frogs.

Being sociable birds, Herons normally nest in colonies known as Heronries, and these are usually to be found towards the tops of some tall trees, always near water. The nests themselves, several of which may be built in one tree, consist of large, rather untidy structures of sticks and twigs which become flattened into huge platforms supporting the shallow cups. These are lined with smaller sticks, twigs, bracken, plant-stems and occasionally grass, though softer materials are seldom used.

Herons have an early breeding season, the eggs being laid sometimes as early as the middle of February, but more usually later in the month or in March. There is normally only one clutch of eggs

Heron

in the year. The number of eggs varies from three to five, and the ground colour is a uniform, beautifully delicate greenish-blue. They are not glossy, and although they bear no markings, they may, like the eggs of so many birds nesting in moist localities, become smeared and stained with damp marks from the sitting bird and from rotting vegetation.

BITTERN

March-June

Botaurus stellaris

Formerly resident in many parts of the British Isles, Bitterns were so severely persecuted that they became virtually extinct for about thirty years until 1911, when nesting birds were once more recorded. Since then a few pairs have bred annually in protected sanctuaries in East Anglia. In other districts Bitterns may occasionally be seen as migrants and winter visitors. They frequent reed beds, being much more often heard than seen. The curious, siren-like call or "boom", several times repeated, and uttered throughout the breeding season, is unmistakable.

The nest is built in dense reed beds : it consists of a heap of reed or sedge, and is rather small for the size of the bird—perhaps about twelve or fourteen inches across the top, though the base is usually broader—but the parent bird, and later the young, gradually flatten it down.

The eggs may be laid at any time from the end of March to the beginning of June. The normally single clutch contains four or five eggs, though more have been recorded. They are a uniform sandy or olive-brown, which makes them very difficult to see against the dead reed or sedge, and they bear no markings.

MUTE SWAN April

Cygnus olor

Mute Swans are widely distributed on rivers, lakes and similar stretches of water.

The nest is built near the water's edge, on a reedy bank or, preferably, on a small island. It is often almost a small island in itself, being a broad mass of reeds, grass and other water-plants, with down lining the cup.

The single clutch of from five to nine eggs is usually laid in April, with each egg approximately $4\frac{1}{2}$ inches long and $2\frac{7}{8}$ inches across—the largest laid by any British nesting bird. In colour the eggs are a uniform greenish-white, unmarked save by damp stains.

GREY LAG GOOSE April

Anser anser

The only truly wild geese to breed in this country, Grey Lags once frequented many districts, but are now confined as residents to the extreme north of Scotland and to some of the Scottish islands. They may also be seen in other districts—chiefly in the west—as winter visitors from September to April. Normally the birds divide their time between open, waste or marshy ground during the day and coastal banks and flats at night.

A scraped hollow in the ground among heather or reeds near water forms the nesting site. The nest itself is built of heather, reeds, twigs or other plant

*Grey Lag
Goose*

stems ; when the eggs are laid a covering of the bird's own down is provided.

From four to six eggs are laid in the single clutch in mid or late April. They are large and white, tinged with yellow or a creamy buff ; they bear no markings other than damp stains.

SHELD DUCK

May

Tadorna tadorna

Widely distributed throughout the British Isles, Sheld Duck are locally abundant. Their haunts are islands, coastal districts, tidal flats, sand-dunes. The nest may occasionally be made in a hollow among rocks, undergrowth at the base of a tree or in a hole in a rotten tree, but is usually in a sandy burrow made either by the birds themselves or, more frequently, by rabbits. The tunnel is widened out at a variable distance from the entrance to form the nest, and is lined with grass, moss and the bird's own down. Several nests close together often form a small colony. Nests are often several miles inland and as soon as the ducklings hatch the duck leads them down to the water.

The single clutch is laid in May and usually contains from six to twelve eggs ; more have been recorded, but larger numbers may have been laid by two birds. The eggs are fairly large and are a uniform creamy white.

MALLARD

March-May

Anas platyrhyncha

Mallard are the most common and widely distributed duck in the British Isles. They frequent marshes, mud-flats, lakes, ponds and reservoirs. During the day they usually rest on the water or along the banks, occasionally swimming or waddling round casually, but they are not really active until the evening, when they fly off in search of food in fields, moors, marshes, ditches, ponds and along the water's edge.

The nesting site is usually a little way from the water, among heather or other thick plants, in hedges, dry reed-beds, in the thick undergrowth of woods or in a hole in a decayed tree several feet above the ground. Reeds, grass, dead leaves and similar materials form the capacious nest and, when the eggs are laid, this is lined with the bird's down, which is used to cover the eggs when the nest is left.

The eggs are laid in a single clutch between March and May, the clutch containing from eight to fourteen eggs. They are variable in colour, ranging from white through cream and buff to a pale greenish-blue or olive-brown, and are unmarked.

GADWALL   May-June

Anas strepera

Better known as winter visitors to the British Isles, Gadwall breed in a few areas, mainly in East Anglia, the Forth Basin and in north-west Ireland. Their haunts are inland (freshwater) lakes and ponds, and their habits are similar to those of Mallard, except that they are generally more retiring. They are also like Mallard in their choice of nesting site, building on dry ground at a little distance from the water's edge. The nest itself is usually well hidden among reeds or other marginal plants, or beneath a low bush. It is built of reeds, grass and similar dry material, and is lined with the bird's down which is lighter than that of Mallard.

There is only one clutch of eggs in the year, laid usually in May, but sometimes in early June. It contains from eight to thirteen eggs, though more have been recorded. They are a uniform and unmarked cream or buff in colour, and are occasionally suffused with a very pale shade of green.

ANATIDAE

TEAL

April-June

Anas crecca

The smallest of our duck, Teal are well-distributed throughout the British Isles, and are also regular and abundant winter visitors. They are more common in northern districts, and particularly in Scotland. In winter, especially when the weather is severe, the birds may be seen on or near tidal estuaries, but they usually frequent inland waters, preferring those whose banks offer plenty of cover. Teal are on the whole more active during the day than most duck, although their main feeding time is from dusk till dawn.

The nesting site is usually a short distance away from the water's edge, among reeds, heather or other plants. There, in a slight hollow, the nest is built of suitable available material—grass, reeds, heather, dead leaves, etc. The usual duck lining of down is in this case very dark in colour.

The eggs are normally laid in the last few days of April or during May, but there may occasionally be late clutches in the first weeks of June. There is only one clutch in the year, and the number of eggs varies from eight to ten, twelve, or even more. The colour is a uniform creamy or buffish-white, sometimes faintly tinged with green, and there are no markings.

GARGANEY

April-May

Anas querquedula

Garganey are summer visitors to the British Isles, arriving from mid-March to the beginning of April and leaving again in late August or during September. They are known only as uncommon migrants in many areas, particularly in Scotland and Ireland, but in a few counties—mostly in the east and south of England —some scattered pairs breed more or less regularly, whilst in Kent and East Anglia they are established, though scarce, summer residents. Their haunts are lakes, ponds and, of course, the Broads. Like most duck, they are more active after dusk than during the day.

Garganey usually choose a nesting site in a marshy situation quite close to the water's edge. The nest, built in a fairly deep depression among reeds, rough grass or other dense marginal plants, consists of grass, reeds, dead leaves and similar materials at hand. The lining of down, which is added after the eggs have been laid, is very dark, but each feather is tipped with a lighter shade.

There is only one clutch of eggs in the year, laid in the last weeks of April or during May. It contains from six to thirteen eggs which are slightly smaller than those of most duck. They are a uniform pale creamy buff, and are unmarked save for stains from damp and rotting vegetation.

WIGEON

April-June

Anas penelope

Common winter visitors to most parts of the British Isles, Wigeon breed only in Scotland. They may frequently be seen in considerable numbers on inland waters, but are really salt-water duck, frequenting bays, estuaries, tidal flats and offshore waters. When undisturbed the birds are often quite active during the day, but, like most surface-feeding duck, feed mainly at night.

The nesting site is among heather, reeds, grass or other plants, usually fairly close to the brink of inland waters. The actual nest is built in a slight hollow in the ground, well shielded by the surrounding plants, or in a clump of reeds or heather. Dry marginal plants form the nesting material, as a rule, and the lining is of sooty-coloured down.

Egg-laying takes place sometime between the last weeks in April and the first weeks in June. There is only one clutch in the year, and it contains from six to ten eggs, though occasionally more are recorded. Their colour ranges from a creamy white to a buffish shade, unmarked save by damp stains.

PINTAIL   April-May

Anas acuta

Pintail are largely confined as residents to certain parts of Scotland and Ireland, but there are a few records of breeding pairs in other areas from time to time. Generally speaking, however, they are regular but not plentiful winter visitors to the British Isles. Their haunts are largely salt-water—inlets, estuaries, tidal flats, and off-shore waters—but although they are seldom found far inland, they do frequent stretches of fresh water near the coast. They feed mainly at night, but are often quite active during the day if undisturbed.

As with most other duck, the nesting site is on the ground near water : Pintail are among those which insist on a dry site. The nest is usually built among plants, but may sometimes be only partially hidden from view. It consists of suitable dry material at hand, and is lined with sooty down.

There is only one clutch in the year, laid in late April or early May, and it contains from seven to ten eggs. They are a uniform yellowish-white in colour, suffused with a pale green.

SHOVELER   April-May

Spatula clypeata

Formerly best known as winter
visitors, Shoveler are increasing as resident birds,
and are now widely,
though still in most
parts sparsely, distri-
buted throughout the
British Isles. They are
most common in parts
of Scotland, Ireland,
Wales and northern
and eastern counties of
England, notably East
Anglia. Though in severe
weather they may be driven
to tidal waters, they usually
frequent inland situations
such as ponds, bogs, marshes, etc.

The nesting site is on or very close to the ground
near water, and Shoveler seem to prefer dry ground,
building among heather, grass or other tangled
growth. When the site is a damp one, a large platform of reeds, grass and other plants will first be
laid, but otherwise the nest is a low structure of dry
plants lined with a dark, almost black, down with
lighter tips.

The eggs are laid in a single clutch in the last days
of April or during May, and number from eight to
twelve. In colour they are a uniform creamy white
or buff, usually tinged with a pale green.

POCHARD   April-June

Aythya ferina

Pochard are largely winter visitors to the British Isles but, like Shoveler, appear to be increasing as resident and breeding birds. They have been recorded as nesting in various localities throughout Great Britain except the south-west. They do not breed in Ireland. Their haunts are chiefly inland, on lakes, reservoirs and gravel-pits, but they may also be seen on coastal waters—bays, inlets, tidal flats and estuaries.

Seldom far from water and sometimes on the very brink, the nesting site is usually a damp one, and consequently the nest itself is frequently raised on a large structure of reeds, grass and other marginal plants. Suitable dry materials form the nest which is lined, often rather sparsely, with blackish down.

The single clutch is laid between the end of April and the beginning of June and contains from six to twelve eggs. These are a uniform buff or creamy grey, usually suffused with a greenish tinge, and are unmarked except where they are stained by damp and rotting plants.

TUFTED DUCK

May-June

Aythya fuligula

At the beginning of this century Tufted Duck were far
from common as resident
and breeding birds in
this country, but are
now firmly established
as such in suitable
localities throughout
the British Isles, whilst
in winter their num-
bers are increased by
visitors from abroad.
They frequent inland
waters, often in large
flocks, and are exceptional
on the coast. Like most
ducks, they are active after
dusk, although they do dive for
food during the day.

The nesting site is generally dry, though never
far from water, and nearly always hidden in a hollow
among surrounding plants or under a bush, but
sometimes it may not be so well concealed. Dry
materials such as grass, reeds and dead leaves form
the nest, which is lined as the eggs are laid with a
darkish down.

There is only one clutch of eggs in the year, laid
in the last weeks of May or during June, and it
numbers from eight to ten and, occasionally, more.
The ground colour is a uniform greenish-grey or
pale olive, and there are no markings apart from
possible damp stains.

COMMON SCOTER

May-June

Melanitta nigra

Abundant visitors to our coasts in winter and at other times, Common Scoter breed very sparingly in the extreme north of Scotland and in one locality in Ireland. Outside the breeding season they are salt-water ducks and may be seen in large flocks off all our coasts in winter.

The nesting site is a hollow in the ground, usually in a damp situation close to the water in marshy scrub or on a small island. The nest itself is well-hidden among the surrounding plants, and consists of suitable dry material—grass, dead leaves, etc.—with a lining of a very dark down added as the eggs are laid.

There is only one clutch of eggs in the year, laid in the last weeks of May or in June. It contains from five to eight or, occasionally, ten eggs, which are a uniform creamy or buffish-white, unmarked except for stains from damp and rotting plants.

GOOSANDER   April-May

Mergus merganser

Goosanders are chiefly winter visitors to the British Isles, but are breeding birds in parts of Scotland (mainly the north) and very occasionally in the extreme north of England. They haunt inland rivers, lakes and reservoirs, and in winter may sometimes be seen on coastal estuaries, inlets and tidal flats. Holes and hollows in trees and banks provide the usual nesting sites, and these are not necessarily on or very close to the ground. A little dry material such as grass or moss forms the scanty nest and the lining consists of a light down.

The single clutch is laid towards the end of April or during May and contains from seven to twelve eggs. These are a uniform cream or very pale buff, and bear no markings.

EIDER DUCK

May-July

Somateria mollissima

Eider Duck breed round the coasts of Scotland, north England and north Ireland. In many areas they appear to be increasing. They are exclusively marine but may occasionally be seen on freshwater lochs near the coast in the breeding season.

The nest, often one of a small colony and seldom far from the coast, is usually well protected by a bush, a rock or the surrounding plants. It consists of grass, heather or seaweed and is plentifully lined with the familiar grey "eider-down."

The single clutch of from four to seven or more eggs is laid between the end of May and the beginning of July ; the large eggs are a uniform greenish colour.

RED-BREASTED MERGANSER   May-June

Mergus serrator

Common residents in suit-
able localities in north and
west Scotland and Ire-
land, Red-breasted
Mergansers are only
winter visitors to
other parts.   As
residents they
frequent both in-
land and coastal
waters, but as visi-
tors they rarely go
inland.

The nesting site
is a hollow in the
ground, seldom far
from water and often
on a small island.   The
nest itself is nearly always
well hidden by the surrounding plants or rocks, and there
may be several nests quite close together.   Each
hollow contains a rather sparse amount of suitable
dry material—grass, heather, dead leaves, etc.—to
which a generous lining of greyish down is added.

There is only one clutch in the year, laid during
May or in early June and containing from six to
twelve eggs.   These are a uniform buff or stone in
colour, and are usually dulled with a slight greyish
or greenish tinge.

CORMORANT   April-May

Phalacrocorax carbo

Cormorants are widely distributed and generally
common around our
coasts, but are scarce
from the Humber to
Sussex. Their haunts
are chiefly coastal
waters and the estu-
aries and bordering
marshes of tidal riv-
ers, but they also fre-
quent some large lakes
and reservoirs.

They usually nest in
colonies on the ledges
of steep coastal cliffs or
among the rocks of small
islands, and occasionally in
trees, especially in Ireland.
These tree nests are built of
sticks and grass and other plants,
but the more usual coastal nests are large structures
of sticks and seaweed.

The single clutch is laid in late April or during
May and contains from three to five eggs. These
are long and slim and a pale blue in colour, but this
is overlaid with a thick chalky deposit, making the
eggs appear white until discoloured by damp seaweed, and rendering them rough to the touch.

PHALACROCORACIDAE

SHAG

Phalacrocorax aristotelis

Very similar to Cormorants in both appearance and habits, Shags are the smaller birds and are not quite so widely distributed. They are most common along the northern and western coasts of Scotland and Ireland and in the Scottish islands, fairly plentiful along the western coasts of England and Wales, but become scarcer in the East. They rarely visit inland waters.

Shags will nest on rocky cliff-faces and in coastal gullies and even caves. The nests are built of wet and often rotting seaweed, and a cave crammed with them has a distinctly strong atmosphere.

The eggs, from two to five in number, are laid from the beginning of April. These are very similar to the Cormorants', though slightly smaller, and, also like them, are blue with a chalky covering which is usually badly stained by the nesting material.

GANNET   April-May

Sula bassana

Gannets, also called Solan Geese, are largely confined as breeding birds to rocky islands round our coasts —mainly off the north of Scotland and the Irish and Welsh coasts. They are sea birds with a strong graceful flight and a powerful dive.

Ledges on steep and craggy rock-faces and, as at Grassholm, the flat top of an island, are packed with nesting birds. The nest consists of seaweed, grass and other plants and often odd scraps of rubbish.

Only one egg is laid in April or May. It is large and in colour a bluish-green overlaid with a rough chalky covering which soon becomes stained.

Storm Petrel   *Leach's Petrel*

STORM PETREL   May-June

Hydrobates pelagicus

Sea-birds for the greater part of the year, Storm
Petrels are established as breeders on rocky islands,
mainly those off the coasts of Scotland, Wales and
Ireland, and off the Scilly Isles.   These petrels,
often called Mother Carey's Chickens, begin to
arrive at the breeding site towards the end of April
and stay there until the young birds can fend for
themselves—usually until the last weeks in August
or the early part of September.

They gather in colonies on the islands, but rarely
make a proper nest.   A hole in a rock or wall, a
space among several rocks or a burrow or depression
in the ground provides the nesting hole, which may
be scantily lined with damp grass.   A noticeable
feature of the site of a Storm Petrel colony is the
strong smell of oil, which comes from the birds'
food.

The single clutch containing only one egg is laid in the last days of May or during June. The egg is a chalky white in colour and bears markings which consist of fine speckles of a reddish-brown shade ; these generally form either a cap or a narrow zone towards the larger end. They are, however, usually rather faint, and may be obscured by damp stains from the nesting hole.

LEACH'S FORK-TAILED PETREL May-June

Oceanodroma leucorrhoa

Very similar in general appearance to Storm Petrels, Leach's Petrels may be distinguished by the clearly forked tail ; they are confined as breeders to a few islands off the northern and north-western coasts of Scotland.

The nesting site and habits are very similar to those of Storm Petrels, except that Leach's are more inclined to burrow in the turf to make the nesting hole.

Slightly larger than the Storm Petrel's, the single egg is laid at about the same time, occasionally a little earlier. It too is a chalky white with a cap or zone of fine reddish-brown speckles at the larger end.

MANX SHEARWATER

May-June

Procellaria puffinus

Manx Shearwaters are no longer to be found in the Isle
of Man, but breed on
various other islands
off the coasts of Scot-
land, Ireland and
Wales, and also in
the Scilly Isles.
They are sea-birds
and, like many of
that kind, move very
awkwardly on land.

They nest in colon-
ies, sometimes in cavi-
ties in rocks or in de-
pressions among loose
stones and soil, but more
generally in burrows which
are either taken over from rabbits
or are excavated by the birds themselves. In the
latter case, the burrows differ considerably in length,
and the eggs may be found at varying distances from
the entrance—sometimes up to about five feet in,
at others within easy hand's reach. There is usually
no nesting material, but occasionally a scanty lining
of grass is provided. The nesting sites are visited
mainly at night, when the sitting birds are relieved
and, after the eggs have hatched, the young are fed.

Only one egg laid, between early May and about
mid-June, and it is white with no markings but
it may sometimes be a little stained.

GREAT CRESTED GREBE
Podiceps cristatus

April-July

Once threatened with extinction through the demand for their " fur," Great Crested Grebes have now, under protection, increased both their numbers and their range. They are now fairly common and widely distributed throughout the British Isles except for the north of Scotland, where they do not breed. They nest on most suitable lakes, meres, reservoirs and gravel-pits. In winter they are frequent in tidal estuaries and coastal waters.

The nest is built at the water's edge, or on the fringe of an island, close to reeds and other marginal plants which serve as anchors for the large floating structure of decaying weeds.

The eggs are laid in a clutch of three or four, and there are often two clutches in the year; laying takes place between April and July. The colour of the eggs is a pale blue or green, but this is over-laid with a chalky deposit which soon becomes badly discoloured by the damp and rotting plants with which the eggs are covered when the parent bird leaves the nest. The unusual shape of the egg is characteristic of the grebes.

LITTLE GREBE   April-June

Podiceps ruficollis

Little Grebes, or Dabchicks as they
are widely known, are quite common on most suitable inland
waters throughout the British
Isles. They are the smallest of
the grebe family and have a
distinctly round appearance.
Ponds, lakes, small reservoirs
and even the slow-moving water
of little-used canals and streams
are their usual haunts; they may
visit estuaries and tidal flats for food,
but remain along the coast only in the
severest weather.

Like their larger relatives, Little Grebes construct
a large floating nest of marginal and water plants,
anchoring the mass to growing plants at the edge of
the water : in very shallow water the nest may be
built up from the bed. The mound of rotting
plants is hollowed at the top to hold the eggs which,
when the sitting bird leaves the nest, are covered
over swiftly and deftly with some of the nesting
material.

There are from four to six eggs in a clutch and
usually two clutches in the year, the first being laid
towards the end of April and the second by the end
of June. The eggs vary in colour from a rather
greyish- or bluish-white to a dull cream, but are
soon heavily stained by the wet rotting nesting-
material which surrounds and from time to time
covers them.

FULMAR

May

Fulmarus glacialis

As late as 1878 Fulmars were known to breed only on St. Kilda, but since then they have spread almost all round the coasts of Britain, except in the south-east (where there are few suitable sites) and along the south coast. They are powerful and graceful sea-birds, seldom coming to land except to breed. Fulmars nest in dense colonies on cliffs and rocky islands, scraping a shallow hollow in the soil or loose surface stones or rock-fragments. The nesting material is scanty and consists of a few bits of grass or other plants or, where these are not to hand, some small flat stones.

The single clutch contains one egg and is laid in May. It has a rough surface and is a uniform white until stained by damp.

COLYMBIDAE

BLACK-THROATED DIVER   May-June

Columbus arcticus

Otherwise known only as winter visitors in small numbers to our coasts, Black-throated Divers breed in the north and west of Scotland but are rare. They are very handsome in their black, grey and white plumage, and are water-birds, moving only very awkwardly on land and, although they have a swift and strong flight, they are seldom on the wing for long periods except when they are on migration. They frequent coastal and inland waters (particularly lochs), where they swim and dive with great speed and power, often pursuing or seeking out fish underwater.

The nesting site is usually close to the water's edge, since the birds cannot walk with any ease, and is often on a small island or strip of ground projecting into the loch : it consists of a shallow depression in the ground or under the shelter of some low plants or bushes. The birds do not usually gather any nesting material and, if they do provide some, it is very slight—a few wisps of grass or other plants forming a scanty lining to the hollow. They breed only on freshwater.

There is only one clutch of eggs in the year : it contains one or, more usually, two eggs which are laid towards the end of May or in the first weeks of June. The ground colour is a darkish and rather dull brown or olive, and the markings consist of black, dark brown and greyish specks, spots and blotches. These are rather sparsely scattered over the shell, but occasionally some may be more thickly clustered at or towards the larger end.

Black-throated Diver

RED-THROATED DIVER
May-June
Colymbus stellatus

Red-throated Divers are more common than their close relatives, mostly as winter visitors to our coasts, but they breed in northern and western Scotland and in northern Ireland in rather small but slowly increasing numbers. Unlike Black-throated Divers they always fish in salt-water, hence they are often seen on the wing in the breeding season, flying to and from the nest, which is always by freshwater, and sometimes several miles from the coast.

The nest is placed quite close to the water's edge in a slight hollow in the turf which is usually unlined except perhaps for a little grass.

The single clutch contains one or two eggs and is laid at the end of May or the beginning of June. The eggs are smaller than those of the Black-throated Diver, but are generally very similar.

Wood Pigeon   *Stock Dove*

WOOD PIGEON   March-September
Columba palumbus

Also called Ring Doves, Wood Pigeons abound in
woods, parks and gardens in town and countryside.

The flat, rather flimsy-looking nest of interwoven
twigs is built at a varying height in a tree or bush.

Two or three clutches are laid, often beginning in
March, with two oval glossy white eggs in each.

STOCK DOVE   March-October
Columba oenas

Stock Doves are perhaps less common but widely
distributed in wooded, open and cliffy country.

Nesting sites are holes in trees, cliffs and buildings, old nests and burrows, with little or no lining.

Laying of the two glossy white eggs begins in
March and there are two or three clutches.

Rock Dove   *Turtle Dove*

ROCK DOVE   March–September

Columba livia

So much interbreeding has occurred with domestic
pigeons which have gone wild that true Rock Doves
are now probably found only on Scottish cliffs and
in Ireland.

The slight nest of twigs, grass and seaweed is on
a ledge or in a crevice of a cave or cliff-face.

The two or three clutches of two glossy white eggs
are laid from March onwards.

TURTLE DOVE   May–July

Streptopelia turtur

Summer visitors chiefly to the south and Midlands,
Turtle Doves breed in thinly wooded country.

The frail-looking nest is usually built in a bush
or low tree.

There are one or two clutches, the first laid in
late May, with two white eggs in each.

WHIMBREL

June

Numenius phaeopus

Otherwise known as " Jack Curlews " from their resemblance to the larger birds, Whimbrels breed only in the Shetland Islands, to which they are summer visitors ; elsewhere in the British Isles they are fairly common birds of passage in spring and autumn. They frequent coastal areas, tidal estuaries, mud-flats and, in the breeding season, rough moors.

The nesting site is among grass, mossy turf or other plants in a slight hollow in the ground. There is no real attempt to build a nest, but a few scraps of dry grass or moss are usually gathered to line the hollow.

The single clutch, laid in June, contains three or four eggs. These are smaller than those of the Curlew, to which, however, they bear some resemblance. The ground colour is a rather pale olive, and the markings consist of specks, spots and blotches of reddish-brown and grey. The eggs are broad at the larger end and more sharply pointed at the smaller than are those of the Curlew.

CURLEW   April-May

Numenius arquata

Curlews are well distri-
buted throughout the
British Isles, al-
though they breed
mainly in Scot-
land, Wales and
northern and
midland Eng-
land, with only
a few pairs nest-
ing on southern
moorlands. They
are usually so-
ciable birds and
may often be seen
in large groups on
or near the feeding
grounds. Their haunts
are tidal estuaries and
mud-flats ; from these the
breeding birds go to inland
moors and upland meadows for
three or four months in the summer. These breeding sites may be well inland, but if they are near the
coast the birds visit their usual feeding grounds
along the shore.

Mossy turf or the ground among clumps of
heather, bracken, reeds, grass or other plants provides the nesting site on the high moors or pastures,
although observations show that the birds seem to

be extending their habitual range to lower ground. There is no real attempt to build a nest in the shallow depression which holds the eggs, but it usually contains a scanty lining of grass, leaves or any suitable similar material which may be to hand.

There is only one clutch of eggs in the year, laid in the last weeks of April or at the beginning of May. It contains three or four, rarely five, eggs, which are broad at the larger end and definitely pointed at the smaller. The ground colour varies from a greenish-buff or yellow to a pale olive shade, and the markings are reddish- and a darker brown. They consist of specks, spots and blotches which are usually scattered rather sparsely over most of the shell, except towards the larger end, where they become more dense, smudging into one another and forming a cap or zone.

WOODCOCK   March-July

Scolopax rusticola

Widely but locally distributed throughout the British Isles, Woodcock are found in almost all suitable localities, though their retiring and largely nocturnal habits may often be the cause of their being overlooked. Their numbers are increased during the winter months by both passage and migrant birds arriving from the end of September, though some of our native birds also move south and west. Woodcock frequent damp woods and coppices where they lie up during the day, rarely showing themselves unless disturbed before dusk, when they seek out marshes, dikes and ditches in search of food.

The nesting site is usually in a wood, where the birds select a hollow in the ground among dead leaves or the shelter provided by bracken or other undergrowth, usually close to the base of a tree. Almost no nesting material is used, what there is consisting of a sparse lining of dry grass, dead leaves, bracken, etc.

Laying may begin as early as March : there are usually two clutches in the year, each containing four eggs laid in a circle with their narrower, pointed ends inwards. The ground colour varies from a creamy white or stone through a rich buff to a pale olive, and is marked with specks, spots and small smudges. These markings are grey and different shades of reddish-brown, and are rather thinly scattered over the shell apart from the larger end, where they are more dense and form a cap.

COMMON SNIPE   March-May
Capella gallinago

Common Snipe are well distributed and often abundant in suitable districts throughout the British Isles. Like Woodcock, they are shy and active mainly after dusk, so their presence may often go unsuspected. Some of our resident birds, again as with Woodcock, migrate southwards in the winter months ; those remaining are joined from October until the end of March by visitors from abroad. The haunts of Common Snipe are marshes and

Woodcock   *Common Snipe*

moorlands, and consequently their numbers as breeding birds are somewhat restricted in southern England.

Moors, marshes and damp ground generally provide nesting sites where the birds select a hollow in the ground and line it with grass. It is always well hidden by surrounding clumps of heather, bracken, reeds or long grass and this, together with the barred and broken pattern of the plumage of the sitting bird, makes a nest almost impossible to detect, even at very close quarters.

The clutch contains four pointed eggs laid in a circle like those of the Woodcock; one or two clutches are produced from March onwards. The ground colour of the eggs is a palish olive, and the specks, spots and smudges are grey and dark brown. These markings often form a spiral pattern.

*Red-necked
Phalarope*   *Dunlin*

RED-NECKED PHALAROPE   June

Phalaropus lobatus

Rarely seen elsewhere in the British Isles, Red-necked Phalaropes are uncommon summer visitors to some of the islands off the northern and western coasts of Scotland and to one district of Ireland, arriving in late May and leaving again at the end of August. They frequent small stretches of inland water usually not far from the coast.

The nesting site, usually quite close to the water's edge, is often in marshy ground. A hollow hidden in the turf or among clumps of marginal plants holds the eggs, a sparse lining of dry grass being all that is usually provided by way of a nest.

The eggs are laid in June in a single clutch of four. The ground colour is a pale olive, plentifully spotted and smeared with a rich dark brown, the markings being most dense at the larger end.

Red-necked Phalaropes reverse the usual order of things : it is the females which pursue the males whilst the latter tend the eggs and chicks.

SCOLOPACIDAE

DUNLIN

May-June

Calidris alpina

Dunlins are amongst the commonest of our waders, haunting the coasts (particularly tidal estuaries with extensive mud-flats) outside the breeding season—indeed some non-breeding birds are usually to be seen in some localities even in midsummer. The birds breed rather sparingly in Wales, the north of England and in parts of Ireland, and more freely in Scotland, particularly in the north and in some of the islands.

High moorlands provide the usual nesting site for Dunlins, but they also nest on lower, marshy ground. The nest, which invariably occupies a shallow hollow in the ground, is usually very well hidden, but occasionally it may be almost completely exposed. It is rather small—little more than three inches in diameter—and is neatly lined with grass, dead leaves or any similar material.

There is only one clutch of eggs in the year, laid towards the end of May or at the beginning of June. It contains four eggs, decidedly pointed at the narrower end, like the eggs of all waders. In colouring and marking they show considerable variation : the ground colour ranges from yellow or buff through green and olive to brown, and the markings from grey and olive to various shades of brown. These markings consist of specks, spots, streaks and smears, usually more dense at the larger end, and sometimes, but not always, following an oblique or spiral direction on the shell.

COMMON SANDPIPER   May-June
Tringa hypoleucos

Well distributed throughout most parts of the British Isles, and abundant in some districts, Common Sandpipers are summer visitors, arriving from the beginning of April and leaving again during September and October. They breed in Scotland, Wales, Ireland and in the northern and extreme western parts of England ; in most of the southern counties, however, they are seen as birds of passage. Breeding birds frequent inland waters—lakes, lochs, rivers and streams—but in late summer they move to the coast, where they remain for a short while before migrating.

The nesting site varies a little, but is almost always quite close to water. It may be near a high moorland tarn or stream, to a lowland pool or river, or in a damp wood : whatever its situation, the nest is nearly always well concealed by the surrounding plants, although some have been found quite un-protected. A hollow in the ground is chosen, and normally lined with grass, dead leaves or other suit-able material, but occasionally this will be either very scanty or missing altogether.

The single clutch contains four eggs, pointed at the narrower end and laid in May or early June. The ground colour is a varying shade of buff, from a creamy tint to a pinkish hue, and the markings are reddish- and dark brown and grey. They consist of specks, spots and smudges and are rather sparsely scattered over the shell, except towards the larger end, where they are a little denser.

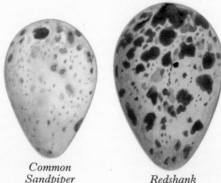

*Common
Sandpiper*

Redshank

REDSHANK   April-May

Tringa totanus

Redshanks are well distributed throughout the
British Isles and are common in many places, but
have decreased in many southern inland localities.
Their numbers are increased at different times by
winter visitors from abroad and by birds of passage.
Their haunts are lakes, marshes and sewage farms
inland and sandy shores and especially tidal estuaries
with extensive mud-flats along the coast.

The sparsely-lined nest is made in a hollow in the
ground not far from water. It is usually but not
always hidden among grass or other plants which the
birds often train over to provide a screen.

The four eggs are laid in a single clutch in April
or May. They vary a little, but usually have a buff
ground colour marked with spots and blotches of
lavender and a rich dark brown.

Ringed Plover

Greenshank

SCOLOPACIDAE

GREENSHANK   May

Tringa nebularia

Known principally in the British Isles as birds of
passage, Greenshanks breed sparsely in northern
Scotland. They frequent lochs in the breeding
season and estuaries and mud-flats on passage.

The nesting site is sometimes close to the water's
edge among grass, heather, reeds or other marginal
plants, occasionally among rocks. Greenshanks also
favour bracken growing round a fallen fir-tree and
the long grass against fences. There is normally
little attempt to build a nest.

There is only one clutch in the year, laid in May
and containing four eggs. The ground colour of
these varies from a light stone through buff to a
pale olive, and the markings of spots, streaks and
blotches, are violet-grey and dark brown or black.

159

CHARADRIIDAE

RINGED PLOVER
April-July

Charadrius hiaticula

Well distributed and fairly common around our coasts, Ringed Plover are resident, though their numbers are increased at times by migrants and, in the winter, by visitors from abroad. They are very sociable birds, and several are usually seen together along the shore, often in a large mixed flock with Dunlins. Their haunts are usually coastal, on sandy and pebbly beaches, but some birds breed inland, especially in Scotland.

The nesting site of Ringed Plover may sometimes be found inland near water, but it is more generally along the shore, among sand or—a favoured spot— the pebbles not far above the high-water mark. The birds make a shallow hollow in the ground and occasionally line it with flat pebbles, a few wisps of grass or pieces of shell or wood. These are fairly inconspicuous against a pebbly background, but when the nest is in sand or turf, the lining may show up quite distinctly.

Laying begins in April, and there are often two clutches in the year. Each clutch will usually contain four eggs although sometimes this may be reduced to three. Like the eggs of most wading birds, these are pointed at the narrower end and are arranged in a circle with the points innermost and sometimes even partially buried in the sand. The ground colour varies from stone to a pale buff or yellow, and the markings—specks and larger spots— are lavender and dark brown or black.

KENTISH PLOVER   May
Charadrius alexandrinus

Kentish Plover used to breed regularly in small numbers in the east and south-east of England. Building developments, assisted perhaps by egg-collectors, sealed the fate of these birds which were probably declining in a natural cycle on the north-western fringe of their range. Certainly since the early 1930's they have ceased to breed regularly, although occasional pairs have bred or have been suspected of breeding. If Kentish Plover are ever to re-establish themselves bird-watchers, as well as egg-collectors, will have to show more restraint and common-sense than they have done in recent years.

The nesting site is occasionally among dry wrack, but is more usually in the sand or among the pebbles above the high-water mark. There is often no nesting-material at all or, at best, a sparse lining of a few pebbles or bits of shell or, more rarely, a few wisps of grass.

There is only one clutch of eggs, laid in May and usually numbering three. They are pointed at the narrower end, which is placed inwards ; as with those of the Ringed Plover, the eggs may be almost vertical with the points buried in the sand or shingle. The ground colour varies from stone to a dull pinkish-buff, and the grey and black markings consist of spots, streaks and scribbles.

Kentish Plover

Golden Plover

GOLDEN PLOVER April-May
Charadrius apricarius

Golden Plover breed in northern England and North Wales and in Scotland and Ireland, mainly on moorland and other high ground. They are fairly common as passage migrants on the coast and as winter visitors to all parts.

The nest is usually in a hollow in the ground, often quite unconcealed by any plants, but it is still difficult to find owing to the broken pattern of the eggs. Little or no lining is provided for the hollow, a few wisps of grass or pieces of moss or heather being the most that is provided.

The single clutch of four eggs may be laid in late April, but is more usual in May. The ground colour varies from stone through buff to a pale olive, and the plentiful markings of spots, blotches and streaks are reddish-brown and black.

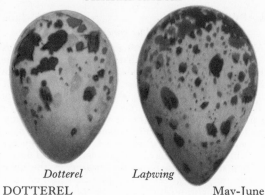

Dotterel   *Lapwing*

DOTTEREL   May-June

Charadrius morinellus

Dotterel are among the rarest of British-breeding birds, being confined to a few of the highest mountains in Scotland. In their best haunts it is sad to relate that they have been persistently harried by egg-collectors but, in recent years especially, expensive protective measures have yielded some good results. Outside the breeding season small flocks or trips are occasionally recorded, sometimes even from sewage-farms close to London.

No real nest is built, the eggs being laid in a bare scrape. As with the Phalarope, the male bird is responsible for incubation and the care of the chicks.

Laying sometimes begins in late May, but more normally the single clutch of three eggs is produced in June. The ground colour ranges from a dirty stone through dusky buff to a pale olive, marked with spots and blotches of grey and deep brown or black.

163

CHARADRIIDAE

LAPWING   April-June

Vanellus vanellus

Also called Green Plovers and Peewits, Lapwings are common and widely distributed throughout the British Isles, and are abundant in some districts. In the winter months they are joined by considerable numbers of visitors from abroad. Their mode of flight and familiar call are characteristic. Their haunts are fairly general over open country—fields, pastures and moorlands inland, and tidal flats, estuaries and beaches along the coast. They are sociable birds and may be seen in large mixed flocks.

The nesting site is on the ground in the open almost anywhere—in rough pasture land or in a ploughed field, on the high slopes of a moor or the lower ground of a marsh. The birds scrape out a shallow depression in the soil and usually line it with a few wisps of grass or straw, pieces of heather etc., though occasionally a half-hearted attempt may be made to build a more substantial nest.

There is only one clutch of eggs in the year, and this is usually laid towards the end of April, occasionally three or four weeks earlier, but agricultural operations sometimes bring disaster to early efforts and replacement clutches may be found in June. Each clutch contains three to five eggs, sharply pointed towards the narrower end, and laid in a circle, points inwards. Shape and size remain constant, but colouring varies greatly, from plain blue to a reddish shade, but more usually the ground colour ranges from a dusky stone or buff to olive, liberally marked with specks, spots and blotches of a very dark brown or black. These markings are usually denser at or towards the larger end.

CHARADRIIDAE

OYSTER-CATCHER   May

Haematopus ostralegus

Also called Sea-pies in some districts, Oyster-catchers have a wide though uneven distribution throughout the British Isles, and their numbers are augmented in winter by visitors from further north. On the eastern and southern coasts of England the birds are far from common, but along the coasts of Wales and north-western England they become more plentiful, and in some parts of Scotland and Ireland they are common. In Scotland and northern England they are breeding inland in steadily increasing numbers.

The nesting site is very variable : often it is among rocks, shingle or sand above the high-water mark on the shore or on a small island, but it may also be on a grassy cliff-top, or even in a field at some little distance from the shore. Inland sites are usually by a river bank or the shore or islet of some mere or loch. The nest also varies considerably : usually it is a slight hollow in the ground, either completely unlined or with a scanty lining of plants, small stones or pieces of broken shell. At times, however, there may be a much more ambitious attempt to line the nest, with plenty of grass, seaweed or other plants.

Laying generally begins early in May, and there is only one clutch, usually containing three eggs, but sometimes four and occasionally only two. The ground colour varies from a creamy stone or buff to a more yellowish shade, and is occasionally suffused with a greenish tinge. The markings are grey and brown or near-black : they are variable, consisting

Oyster-catcher

of a mixture of specks, spots, streaks, blotches and scribbles scattered evenly over the shell, or sometimes clustered more densely towards the larger end.

LITTLE RINGED PLOVER   May

Charadrius dubius

Little Ringed Plovers first bred in England in 1938. Since then they have steadily increased and, though still rare, may now be considered to have established themselves in the south and south-east. They breed by inland gravel-pits, reservoirs and, rarely, by stony streams.

Avocet *Sandwich Tern*

RECURVIROSTRIDAE

AVOCET April-June

Recurvirostra avosetta

One of the happiest events in ornithology for many years has been the re-establishment of the beautiful Avocets as British-breeding birds. After an absence of over a century a few pairs bred in Suffolk in 1947. Thanks to the efforts of the Royal Society for the Protection of Birds, there is now a flourishing colony on the Society's bird reserve on Havergate Island.

Nests vary, sometimes consisting of only a thinly-lined scrape, but often being of a more substantial nature. Occasionally the nest of a Black-headed Gull is usurped.

Only one clutch is laid in the year, and it usually contains four eggs, but sometimes five may be laid or occasionally only three. The eggs are usually dark buff or stone in the ground colour and are liberally blotched with dark brown.

LARIDAE

SANDWICH TERN   May

Sterna sandvicensis

Sandwich Terns are summer visitors from April to September. They nest in widely scattered colonies, mainly along our eastern coasts.

The nesting site is usually among sand dunes, on a sand or shingle beach, or in reedy and sedgy surroundings, sometimes by freshwater but never far from the sea. The birds nest in colonies or in small groups, sometimes among a colony of other terns or of gulls. The nest itself may be nothing more than a slight unlined depression, or it may be a little deeper, with a scanty lining.

There is only one clutch of eggs in the year, laid in May and containing from one to three eggs. The ground colour ranges from a creamy white or stone to a rich buff, and is marked with specks, spots and blotches of grey, brown and black.

BURHINIDAE

STONE CURLEW April-June

Burhinus oedicnemus

Also known in different districts as Norfolk
Plovers and Thick-knees, Stone Curlews are summer visitors to the British Isles. The majority of
birds, however, arrive from the end of March and
leave again during October. They are found only
in East Anglia and southern England and their numbers are slowly diminishing, due mainly to intensive
agriculture and the afforestation of many suitable
areas. After the nesting season the birds become
sociable and sometimes gather in large flocks. They
are seldom to be seen during the day, but become
active after dusk. They favour open country such
as commons, heaths, downs and shingle beaches of
wide extent.

Such situations provide the nesting site, where a
shallow hollow is scratched in the ground, which
may often be bare of surrounding plants, although
stony soil is usually preferred if available. There is
little or no attempt to furnish even a lining for the
nest, but when the birds do decide to provide one
they often make the rather odd choice of a collection of rabbit droppings.

The eggs are often laid towards the end of April,
sometimes during May and, less frequently, at the
beginning of June. There is normally one clutch
in the year and this usually contains two eggs. The
ground colour of these varies from stone to buff, and
the markings are different shades of grey and brown.
They vary considerably : consisting mainly of spots,
blotches, lines and streaks, they may in some specimens be mixed and scattered more or less evenly

Stone Curlew

over the shell, but in others there may be only spots and blotches, or even simply a sketchy network of lines.

Few birds are more striking than Stone Curlews when seen at close quarters : they seem almost to transfix one with their staring, yellow eyes. They are, however, shy birds as a rule, seldom permitting really close approach and at a distance their plumage harmonises with their general surroundings so well that they can be easily overlooked. After the breeding season they often gather into large flocks, sometimes up to one hundred strong, prior to migration.

Roseate Tern   Common Tern

ROSEATE TERN   May-June

Sterna dougallii

Roseate Terns are summer visitors to some of the coasts and islands around the British Isles, arriving towards the end of April and leaving again during August. They are far from common, probably for two reasons : severe persecution in the past, both for plumage and for eggs, and competition for nesting sites with larger gulls, many of which begin the breeding season a little earlier in the year. They are sea-birds, coming to land mainly only for breeding purposes, and then they frequent rocky coasts and islands.

The nesting colony is usually found in such places, surrounded by the colonies of other terns and gulls ; very occasionally, however, a site may be chosen among sand-dunes or on coastal flats. There is little or no attempt to provide even a lining, still less a nest, and the eggs are usually laid in a hollow or on a ledge among the rocks.

There is only one clutch of eggs in the year, generally laid in late May or June. It sometimes contains two eggs, but one is more usual. The ground colour varies from a light stone to buff and occasionally a darker shade, and the markings, which may be specks, spots or blotches, are varying shades of grey and brown, and sometimes form a zone towards the larger end.

COMMON TERN   May-June
Sterna hirundo

Summer visitors, arriving in April and leaving in October, Common Terns are widely distributed around the coasts of the British Isles, though they are less common in the north. Their haunts are largely coastal, but they also visit tidal rivers and may even be seen occasionally inland.

The nesting site for the colony or ternery, as it is called, is generally among sand dunes or shingle above the high-water mark, but may also be among rocks or on saltings : islands are often favoured. Sometimes little or no material is used to line the nest, but there is usually a collection of sprigs of plants mixed with shells and other shore litter.

Two, sometimes three, eggs are laid in the single clutch. The ground colour ranges from a pale buff through olive to brown, and the markings are various shades of grey, brown and black. They consist of specks, spots and blotches, sometimes scattered rather sparsely over the shell, but in other cases grouped in broad zones, often with a cluster of blotches forming a cap at the larger end.

ARCTIC TERN June
Sterna macrura

Like all terns summer visitors to the British Isles,
Arctic Terns are most common along the northern
shores of Scotland and Ireland, where they largely
replace Common Terns, but elsewhere their colonies
are few. They arrive in late April or early May,
leaving again in October, and frequent the coast and
sometimes inland waters.

The nesting colony may be sited among rocks or
sand dunes, on shingle, often on a small island off-
shore or by an inland lake. Some attempt may be
made to furnish a sparse lining for the nesting hollow, but the eggs are often laid on the bare ground.

The single clutch of two or, less frequently, three
eggs is laid in June. The ground colour ranges from
stone through buff to an olive-brown, and the spots
and blotches are grey and a very dark brown. Like
those of the Common Tern, the eggs are very variable
in colour and marking.

LITTLE TERN May-June
Sterna albifrons

Little Terns are, as their name suggests, the smallest
of their kind to visit the British Isles, and are perhaps
the most charming of a family of birds delightful in
all but their voices. Summer visitors, Little Terns
arrive from about the middle of April and during
May, and most of them have left our shores by the
end of September. They are widely distributed
around our coasts, except in the extreme north of
Scotland, but they are local, and common only in a
few places.

173

Arctic Tern   *Little Tern*

Like other terns, these birds nest in colonies, but
these are generally quite small, with the individual
nests well scattered, and are only very rarely found
among rocks. The usual site is among the stretches
of sand or shingle above the high-water mark, but
grassy flats are avoided. The nests are sometimes
placed dangerously near the water's edge, and a particularly high tide may well sweep the whole colony
away. Sometimes the eggs are laid straight on to the
ground with no preliminary scrape to receive them,
but usually a slight hollow is made, which may be
lined with broken shell or small stones.

There is only one clutch of eggs in the year, laid
in mid-May or early in June, although if the first
meets with disaster a second clutch is usually laid to
replace it. The clutch contains two, three or, more
rarely, four eggs, which are considerably smaller
than those of other terns. The ground colour is a
greyish-white or pale buff, marked with specks,
spots and smears of grey and brown.

BLACK-HEADED GULL   April-May

Larus ridibundus

There are two anomalies concerning Black-headed Gulls : one is that the " black " of the head is really brown, the other that they are in many parts the commonest of British gulls, and yet the name " Common Gull " belongs to another bird. Black-headed Gulls are generally well distributed throughout the British Isles, and have become perhaps the least " sea-minded " of gulls, for although they frequent estuaries and the coast, they also follow the rivers back inland and are often seen over fields and sewage farms far from the coast. Like most gulls, these birds are extremely sociable, and may be seen in large numbers both inland, with Rooks, Lapwings and Golden Plovers, and on the coast, with parties of other gulls and with many of the wading birds.

They are also, like most gulls and terns, very sociable in the breeding season, and nest in large colonies or gulleries. The site for these is usually close to the water : above the high-water mark on the shore, by the edge of water inland, on an island off-shore or in a lake or mere, on saltings or an inland marsh—these are all favoured places. The nest itself is usually built on the ground but it may sometimes be on a wall or a rocky ledge. It consists of a collection of sticks, grass, reeds, sedges and similar material in the vicinity, lining a depression in the ground if this is dry, but where the surroundings are very damp it may become quite a large structure.

There is only one clutch of eggs in the year, and it is laid towards the end of April or sometime during May. It contains two or three eggs, though in rare cases four have been recorded. There is considerable variation both in the colour and in the marking of the eggs. The ground colour ranges from a creamy buff through bluish and greenish shades to olive and brownish, and the markings are grey with different shades of brown to near-black. These markings consist of spots and blotches, which are often scattered more or less evenly over the shell, although they may sometimes be clustered together in a zone.

COMMON GULL   May-June

Larus canus

Common Gulls are somewhat mis-named, for in most parts of the British Isles the commonest members of the family are either the Black-headed or the Herring Gulls. As all-the-year-round residents Common Gulls are restricted to Scotland and the north of Ireland, where they are often abundant. To most other districts of Britain they are visitors outside the breeding season, arriving in August and September and leaving again in March, but there is one precarious and isolated breeding colony in the south of England. In the breeding season they are always to be found on or near the coast, but in winter they feed freely inland.

The usual site for the nest is on shingle, often on a beach quite close to the high-water mark. A crevice among rocks or a hollow scraped in the ground generally furnishes the site for the nest itself, but on the moors a thick clump of grass or heather may hold it. Little nesting material is used, a scrappy collection of bits of grass, heather, seaweed or other plants being the usual lining.

Laying begins about the middle of May, and there is only one clutch in the year. This contains two or, more frequently, three eggs, and these show considerable variation in both colour and marking. The

Common Gull

ground colour ranges from a pale buff through greenish-blue to a brownish-olive, and the markings are grey, brown and near-black. They consist of spots, blotches and smears, and are usually scattered rather sparsely over the shell, but may occasionally be more dense. Completely unmarked bluish eggs have also been recorded.

HERRING GULL

April-May

Larus argentatus

Widely distributed in coastal areas throughout the British Isles, Herring Gulls are plentiful in many districts except the south-east, and they frequently rival Black-headed Gulls in abundance. They are increasing in numbers and whereas formerly they were largely confined to coastal areas, they now breed inland as well. They frequent the shore, tidal estuaries, harbours and cultivated land near the coast.

The colony of nests is usually built on the rocky ledges or grassy slopes of steep cliffs, but also on the turf of small islands or even on a moor near the sea. The nest itself is often concealed and protected by the surrounding plants or rocks, although it may sometimes be more exposed. It is normally a rather shallow and untidy structure of grass, heather, roots, seaweed or other plants, generally on the ground, but sometimes on a low rock or wall. There may be a slight lining of sheep's wool.

There is only one clutch of eggs in the year, laid towards the end of April or at the beginning of May. It contains three eggs normally, although sometimes there may be only two. The ground colour ranges from buff through a yellowish-olive to olive-brown, marked with grey and shades of brown to near-black. These markings are variable : they consist of specks, spots and blotches which in some specimens are rather sparsely scattered over the shell, but in others are more plentiful.

LESSER BLACK-BACKED GULL April-May

Larus fuscus

There are two races of Lesser Black-backed Gulls, the British and the Scandinavian, the latter being noticeably darker on the upper parts. Birds of the British race breed in this country but move south in the winter, being replaced by birds of the Scandinavian race. They are widely distributed around our shores, but rather locally, the main colonies being in the north-east of England, along the western shores of England and Wales, and in Scotland and Ireland. Like Herring Gulls they can be seen inland, but are more generally coastal birds, with tidal estuaries, harbours, coastwise fields and the sea off-shore as their usual haunts.

The birds nest occasionally on cliffs, but grassy slopes or islands, marshes or moors are usually chosen. The nest itself may sometimes be merely a scrape in the ground or turf with no lining at all, but generally it resembles that of the Herring Gull, though sometimes a little smaller. Grass, seaweed and other plants are the usual nesting materials.

Laying begins at the end of April or in the first weeks of May and there is only one clutch in the year. This contains two or three eggs which, like

Lesser Black-backed Gull

those of other members of the family, vary somewhat in both colour and marking. The ground
colour may be stone or buff—sometimes tinged with
green—or olive-brown or green. The markings
consist of specks, spots and blotches of grey, reddish-
brown and near-black, and may be either sparsely or
more plentifully scattered over the shell.

GREAT BLACK-BACKED GULL   May-June

Larus marinus

Unlike their smaller relatives, Great Black-backed Gulls are resident in the British Isles, though not in all districts. As breeding birds they are compara- tively plentiful in Scotland and the islands off the

Scottish coasts, in parts of northern and western Ireland, in Wales and western and southern England. In winter, however, they may be seen in nearly all coastal districts and immature birds are present on all coasts throughout the summer. They rarely go inland, being mainly confined to estuaries, the shore and coastal waters.

These birds are increasing in numbers, often to the detriment of their weaker brethren, and though they are not really colonial in habit several pairs may often be found breeding close to each other. Rocky cliffs and small islands are the usual nesting sites, while the nest itself consists of an untidy mass of grass, seaweed, thrift and similar plants, together with sticks and other rubbish which may be at hand.

There is only one clutch of eggs in the year, laid during May or at the beginning of June. The eggs number two or three and are the largest produced by members of the gull family. The ground colour ranges from stone or buff, often tinged with greenish-grey, to olive, and bears markings of grey, brown and near-black. These markings consist of specks, spots and blotches which are seldom very plentiful and may sometimes be clustered mainly towards the larger end.

KITTIWAKE

May-June

Rissa tridactyla

Kittiwakes are confined largely to the northern and western coasts of the British Isles, being abundant in suitable districts of Scotland and Ireland and plentiful though very local along the shores of Wales and of western England ; on the east they do not breed south of the Humber, probably through lack of suitable sites. They are among the smallest members of the family, being scarcely larger than the Black-headed Gulls, and are also the most truly oceanic, for except in the summer months they frequent the open sea well away from land. In the breeding season they come to steep shore cliffs and rocky islands around our coasts, congregating in March and early April in large colonies.

These sites are usually crowded with birds, and the nests are more usually placed on ledges or in crevices. So narrow are some of these, and so apparently flimsy some of the nests, that the latter appear to be in constant danger of being blown or knocked down on to the rocks beneath. In fact, however, the nest is a very strong structure of grass and seaweed mixed with mud and clay, the whole being trodden together to form a firm base. On this more grass and seaweed may be heaped until the cup

Kittiwake

for the eggs rests on a large mass, but many nests are quite compact.

The single clutch of eggs contains two or three eggs and is usually laid during May, though some may be as late as the first weeks of June. The ground colour is lighter than that of most gulls' eggs, being normally a greyish-stone or buff. The markings of specks, spots and blotches are grey and a dark reddish-brown, and, although varying a little in number, are seldom very dense, but may be grouped in zones.

ARCTIC SKUA   May-June

Stercorarius parasiticus

Sometimes called Richardson's Skuas, Arctic Skuas are chiefly summer visitors to parts of the British Isles, but in spring and autumn they may be seen over other (notably eastern) coasts on passage. They are confined as breeding birds to the far north of Scotland and to some of the islands off the northern Scottish coasts, notably the Orkneys, Shetlands and Hebrides. Like their larger relatives they are principally sea-birds, with the seas between

the southern Atlantic and the Arctic as their haunts.
In the summer months the visiting birds may be
seen over moorland and near the coast, where they
pursue the smaller gulls and terns and force them
to yield their catch of food.

Arctic Skuas nest in colonies, but these are scattered with the nests usually widely separated ; the
colonies are sited on moors. The birds make no real
attempt to build a nest, but generally scrape a hollow
in the turf or trample the centre of a clump of
heather or grass. There may be a sparse lining of
grass or other plants, but often the depression is
completely unlined. These birds are among those
which will feign injury to distract attention from the
nest, although they will also attack intruders by
swooping at them.

There is only one clutch of eggs in the year, laid
towards the end of May or in the first weeks of June.
It normally contains two eggs which are similar to
though smaller than those of the Great Skua. The
ground colour is some shade of olive-brown or
green, sometimes smudged here and there with a
blackish-grey. The markings, which are seldom
very plentiful, consist of specks, spots, smudges and
scribbles of reddish-brown and near-black.

GREAT SKUA   May-June

Stercorarius skua

Great Skuas, at one time in danger of extinction, have generally increased in the Shetlands and now breed also in the Orkneys. But they do not breed anywhere else, though they may occasionally be seen on our coasts, passing to and from their northern breeding-grounds, which they leave at the end of the summer.

The site for the nesting colony is often a peat-moor and here the first birds return at the end of March or early in April, although the first eggs are not laid for another month. As with the Arctic Skua, the nests are scattered over a wide area with plenty of space between. A hollow scraped in the ground or a depression made in a clump of plants serves as the nesting site, whilst the nest itself is seldom more than a sparse lining of grass or other plants. On entering the nesting-grounds, especially during that period when the eggs are hatching or when the chicks are about, the bird-watcher will find himself subjected to an impressive series of mock-attacks. The adults have two forms of attack, one at a low level, the bird flying in at the intruder at the level of his face, banking up steeply and flying over him with a swish of wings ; the other takes the form of dive-bombing, the bird sweeping down at the intruder from some height and at a steep angle, gaining considerable speed and turning away only when within a few feet. As this bird is a big one, a first experience of these attacks is likely to prove disconcerting and more than one bird-watcher has been forced to beat a hasty and ignominious retreat. Actually there is no danger at all ; the attacks are

Great Skua

only very rarely pressed home and the very worst
the observer will get may be a sharp flip from a
wing, no more damaging than being hit smartly over
the head by a piece of thin cardboard.

Laying usually takes place during the last weeks
of May, but sometimes the single clutch of eggs is
not produced until the beginning of June. It contains two largish eggs, the ground colour of which
varies from a dusky buff to olive or olive-brown.
The markings are grey, reddish-brown and near-
black and consist of spots, blotches and smears.
They are seldom plentiful, being thinly scattered
over the whole shell.

RAZORBILL

May-June

Alca torda

For most of the year Razorbills are sea-birds, spending their time well away from land, which they seldom visit unless driven ashore by storms. From the end of February onwards they begin to come inshore for the breeding season, frequenting coastal waters.

Then in April and May they congregate, usually in large numbers, on rocky cliffs and islands, often in company with their relatives the Guillemots, and there is much fuss and quarrelling over the choice of sites. They are widely but locally distributed around the coasts of the British Isles, except in England south of Flamborough Head and east of the Isle of Wight.

The sometimes huge colonies crowd steep, craggy cliffs which are their usual site, though lower rocky islands are also chosen. The birds make no attempt to build a nest, the eggs being laid on to the bare rock, sometimes in a crevice, but often dangerously near the edge of the rocky platform.

There is only one clutch in the year, laid towards the end of May, and it contains one large egg which varies a great deal in both colour and marking. The ground colour ranges from off-white through cream, buff and greenish- or bluish-yellow to a light reddish-brown, and the markings are grey, reddish-brown and black. They comprise specks, spots, smudges, blotches, streaks and lines in almost any combination and in varying density.

GUILLEMOT

May-June

Uria aalge

Guillemots have almost an identical distribution to the Razorbill but are certainly more numerous, though there is some evidence of a decline in numbers, especially in the south. Some birds have a white ring round the eye and a thin white strip extending backwards from it. These so-called " bridled " birds are much commoner in the north than the south.

Certainly in the south of Britain, Guillemots and Razorbills are decreasing in numbers. It is not easy to account for this decline, but it is true that both these species, and especially the Guillemot, suffer heavily from the effects of oil-pollution. This miserable and cruel death, in which the victim gets its plumage so heavily clogged with foul oil that it loses buoyancy and the ability to dive and fly, slowly dying of starvation, accounts for thousands of these birds every winter. This is known from surveys undertaken by the Royal Society for the Protection of Birds, which has been fighting the menace of oil-pollution for many years.

The vast colonies throng the rocks and ledges of steep cliff faces, often in company with large numbers of Razorbills, from which they are distinguishable by their more upright stance. There is no attempt at nest building, and the eggs are laid on the bare rock, where their position is extremely precarious.

Laying takes place in May, usually towards the end of the month, and there is only one clutch in the year. This contains a single egg which is large and

Guillemot

pointed at the narrower end. As with the Razorbill's egg, there is considerable variation in both colour and marking. The ground colour may be anything from white through cream, yellow and buff to shades of green, blue, reddish, purplish and brown, and the markings similarly vary in colour. They consist of different combinations of specks, spots, blotches, streaks and lines, occasionally clustered mainly towards the larger end, but seldom very dense.

Above : *Puffin*

Below : *Black Guillemot*

ALCIDAE

BLACK GUILLEMOT
May-June
Uria grylle

Black Guillemots are confined as breeding birds largely to the coasts of Scotland and Ireland, to the Isle of Man and some islands off the Scottish shores ; further south they are rare winter visitors. They come inshore near rocky cliffs from the open sea from February onwards.

The colonies are usually small, and no nests are built, the eggs resting in a crevice in a cliff-face, among rocks or in a rabbit-hole.

The eggs are laid in a single clutch of two in late May or early June. The white, creamy or faintly green ground colour bears specks, spots and blotches, usually denser at the larger end, of lavender-grey and dark or reddish-brown.

PUFFIN
May-June
Fratercula arctica

Also called Sea-parrots, Puffins are widely distributed on suitable coasts around the British Isles, though most abundantly in the west, Wales, Scotland and Ireland. They are sea-birds, coming to land from March onwards only for the breeding season, when they frequent cliff-slopes and rocky islands.

There the huge colonies throng grassy, sandy or rocky cliffs, where a crevice or hole among rocks or a burrow in the sand—a rabbit-hole is a favourite choice—holds the nest. This may be unlined, or have an untidy collection of damp grass, seaweed, feathers, etc.

The single egg is laid in late May and is white, faintly spotted with sub-surface markings of reddish-brown or grey but it soon bears damp stains.

CORNCRAKE
May-June

Crex crex

Summer visitors to the British Isles, Corncrakes or
Land-rails arrive towards the end of April or in May
and leave again during September and October.
Their numbers have greatly decreased and they are
now common only in parts of Scotland and Ireland.
They seldom breed in southern or midland England,
Their breeding haunts are long grass and hayfields.
but they are seldom seen, although their rasping
double call, monotonously repeated, at once reveals
their presence.

The nesting site may sometimes be in damp
situations, among reeds or sedge, but is more usually
in grass and, where this is being grown for hay, the
chicks are often destroyed during mowing. The nest
itself is simply a hollow in the ground, lined with a
little grass and sometimes having the surrounding
grass drawn over to help concealment.

Laying begins in May with normally only one
clutch of from seven to ten or more eggs, but if the
first is destroyed a second is usually produced. The
ground colour is a creamy or slightly pinkish-buff,
sparsely marked with reddish-brown spots and
blotches.

WATER-RAIL
April-June

Rallus aquaticus

Water-rails are resident in suitable districts throughout the British Isles, except in the north of Scotland
and the Scottish islands, but they are such shy birds
that little is known for certain about their distribution ; their numbers are increased by winter visitors

Corncrake   *Water-rail*

from abroad. They frequent marshes, reed-beds
and similar damp situations, where they hide among
the dense water-plants.

In such wet places is the nesting site, the nest itself being very well concealed by the surrounding
plants. It usually rests on a platform of broken
plant-stems, which lifts it out of the water, and is
built of reeds, sedge, grass or any other similar
material in the vicinity.

The first clutch of eggs is laid in April and is often
followed by a second, each containing between six
and twelve eggs. The ground colour ranges from a
slightly pinkish-stone through buff to a pale brown,
and bears specks and spots of grey, reddish-brown
and near-black. These markings are never very
plentiful, and may be scattered evenly over the shell
or mainly clustered towards the larger end.

MOORHEN   March-July

Gallinula chloropus

The most common and widely distributed members of the family, Moorhens may be seen on almost any suitable stretch of inland water. Their name has no connection with moorlands, but is a corruption of Merehens and they are also called Waterhens. They are found throughout the British Isles on ponds, lakes, meres, marshes and rivers fringed with dense marginal plants. Although chiefly waterbirds they visit fields at some distance for food to supplement their aquatic diet.

The nesting site is amongst the marginal plants or in a bush, usually but not invariably close to the water's edge. When built on the ground the nest is usually well hidden, but may sometimes be exposed. It is compact and rather flat, consisting of interwoven grass, reeds, etc., lined with softer material. When built in a bush it often rests on the old nest of some other bird.

There are two and sometimes three clutches in the year, each containing from six to ten or even twelve eggs; the first is usually laid in April, although March eggs have been recorded. The ground colour of the eggs is a creamy or pinkish-buff speckled and spotted with lavender-grey and reddish- or a darker brown. These markings are seldom very dense but are scattered over the whole shell.

SPOTTED CRAKE
May-June

Porzana porzana

Spotted Crakes are summer visitors arriving from March onwards and leaving again during October. They breed sparingly and very locally in England and Wales, but they are so retiring and skulking in their habits that it is seldom possible to prove breeding, the presence of the birds usually being revealed only by their calls.

The nest is built close to water, supported by a clump of turf or by broken plant-stems, and is usually screened by the surrounding plants. Reeds and other water-plants are interwoven to contain the lining of softer material.

The single clutch of from eight to twelve eggs is laid in May or early June. They are not unlike those of the Corncrake (*q.v.*), except that the buff ground colour is usually more olive, and the markings are sometimes darker.

COOT
March-July

Fulica atra

Somewhat similar to Moorhens, Coots are as widely distributed throughout the British Isles, but are less common than the smaller birds, and tend to move southwards in the winter months. They are water-birds and meres, lakes, marshes and rivers are their haunts.

Plants at the water's edge conceal the nest, which is a large structure that the birds raise by adding

Coot

more material if the water-level rises. It is built of reeds, sedge and other marginal plants with a softer lining.

There are two and sometimes three clutches in the year, with from six to ten or even twelve eggs in each. Laying may begin in March but is more usual in April. The ground colour is a variable shade of stone or buff, marked with dark brown or black. These markings consist of fine specks, interspersed with a few slightly larger spots, all scattered evenly over the whole shell.

TETRAONIDAE

CAPERCAILLIE   April-June

Tetrao urogallus

Capercaillie, or Wood Grouse as they are sometimes called, have an interesting history. They are believed to have been native birds originally, but disappeared several centuries ago, first from England and Wales, then later from Scotland and Ireland as

203

well. The reason for this disappearance is obscure, although the destruction of forest areas may have been partially responsible. In 1837, the birds were re-introduced to the British Isles from Sweden. The place chosen was in the neighbourhood of Perth, and from here the birds have spread until they are now well distributed through many forest areas of central Scotland, notably those growing pine trees, although deciduous woods are also frequented.

The nesting site is on the ground in a wood, beneath a tree or shrub, or amongst low under-growth, and there a shallow depression is scraped out in the soil. This may be used as it is, but the birds usually line it, though often rather sketchily, with pine needles and bits of moss, grass, heather or similar material.

Laying begins towards the end of April or during May, and there is only one clutch of eggs in the year. This contains any number from six to eight, ten, or even more, largish eggs. There is little variation in colour or marking, the ground colour being sandy or yellowish-buff marked with a deeper sandy shade through to chestnut. The markings are evenly distributed over the whole shell, and consist of specks and spots occasionally interspersed with small blotches.

TETRAONIDAE

BLACK GROUSE   April-June

Lyrurus tetrix

Unknown in Ireland, Black Grouse are widely but unevenly distributed throughout the rest of the British Isles. They are rarely seen in the eastern and southern counties of England, and are very local in western and south-western districts and in Wales. In Scotland and northern England they are more plentiful, although still only in certain areas. The males, or Black-cock, are easily identified at most times of the year by their lyre-shaped tails and glossy black plumage, but the females, or Grey-hens, are less spectacular in appearance. Their haunts are thinly wooded moors, cultivated land and, in the north, denser woodlands.

The display of the Black-cock is one of the most astonishing sights in ornithology. The males gather at the display-ground or " lek," where each stakes out a particular piece of ground or " territory," from which he drives other males and struts around, raising and lowering head and neck, flapping his wings, fanning his tail, often jumping up and down in what appears to be a frenzy of excitement. It is in this way that the males attract the females and mate with them. Favoured " leks " are resorted to year after year, but the birds usually display only very early in the morning or, to a lesser degree, at sunset.

Black Grouse seldom nest in the heart of a forest, but choose as nesting sites the outer fringes of woods and plantations, copses bordering a moor or the open moorland itself. The nest consists of a scrape in the ground at the foot of a tree, beneath a low bush or

Black Grouse

among dense undergrowth, bracken or heather. This usually has a sparse lining of grass, heather, leaves or bits of other plants.

There is only one clutch of eggs in the year, laid either in the last weeks of April or during May. It contains from six to ten, and sometimes more, eggs, which bear a strong resemblance to those of the Capercaillie, although they are noticeably smaller. Like those, they have a buff ground colour which is suffused with a yellowish or sandy tinge, but the markings are often a richer shade of reddish-brown. They comprise specks, spots and small blotches which are scattered evenly but rather thinly over the whole shell.

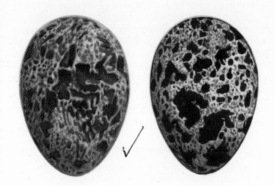

Red Grouse   *Ptarmigan*

RED GROUSE   April-June

Lagopus scoticus

Widely distributed throughout Scotland, Wales, northern England and Ireland, Red Grouse are game-birds and frequent moorland, generally about 1,000 feet or more above sea-level, although in severe weather they will often move to lower ground. They are the only truly British game-birds : attempts have been made to introduce them on the Continent.

The nesting site is among heather, bracken, grass or other moorland plants. Here the birds scrape a hollow in the ground, and this is sparsely lined with sprigs of grass, heather or similar material and perhaps a few feathers ; the hollow is usually well screened by the surrounding plants.

Towards the end of April or during May the single clutch is laid, containing from six to ten eggs, although more are sometimes found. The ground colour is a creamy, yellowish- or pinkish-buff, liberally marked with a rich reddish- or darker brown. These markings consist of spots, mottles and blotches more or less evenly distributed over the whole shell.

PTARMIGAN   May-June

Lagopus mutus

Ptarmigan are confined as British breeders to the highlands of Scotland, usually nesting on high ground above the 2,500-ft. contour ; in the winter months, when their plumage is almost entirely white, making them inconspicuous against the snow, the birds will often gather in large flocks and descend to slightly lower levels. Their haunts are not moorlands, but rocky slopes and mountain tops where plant-life is sparse.

In such places is the nesting site, the nest itself being little more than a bare scrape in the soil, for there is little if any lining—a few wisps of grass usually being the most that is provided.

The single clutch is laid during May or early in June, and contains from seven to ten eggs. These are very similar to those of the Red Grouse, but the ground colour is usually less warm, and the markings are often darker.

PHEASANT   April-June
Phasianus colchicus

Familiar and widely distributed throughout the
British Isles, Pheasants are common in many districts. Strictly speaking, they are not native birds,
but as they were first introduced at least a thousand
years ago, they are usually admitted as being
naturalised by now ! They are semi-domesticated,
for they are game-birds and therefore carefully
watched over and tended. From time to time different types have been introduced and cross-bred,
so that most of our birds are now an extremely
mixed collection. They frequent wooded districts
where there is plenty of thick cover.

The nesting site is amongst such cover : under
the protection of a dense bush or bramble, or in
thick grass, a hollow is made which is lined—usually
rather sketchily—with a few wisps of grass and some
dead leaves.

There is only one clutch of eggs in the year, laid
towards the end of April or during May. The number it contains is variable and, although ten or twelve
are very common, there may be as few as seven or as
many as eighteen. They are usually rather broadly
rounded at the larger end and are an unmarked
olive-brown in colour.

PARTRIDGE   April-July
Perdix perdix

Partridges too are game-birds, and as such are also
preserved, although somewhat less intensively than
Pheasants. They are widely distributed in suitable
districts throughout the British Isles, though not

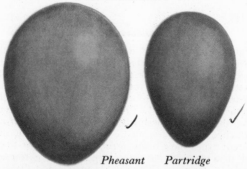

Pheasant   Partridge

plentiful in Ireland ; in some places they are called Grey Partridges. Their haunts are generally culti- vated fields, though they are also found on higher pasture land and on the lower moors and, less fre- quently, on marshes and sand-dunes. They are sociable birds and the families do not split up when the young birds have grown, but spend the winter together, often with other parties, in flocks known as coveys.

The dense growth of hedges, bushes and the weeds bordering an open field provide nesting sites where the nest itself will be well concealed. It con- sists of a depression amongst such plants, or a hollow in the ground, which is lined with leaves and grass, the leaves being drawn over the eggs when the parent bird is off the nest.

The single clutch of eggs is laid from the end of April onwards, and contains any number between seven and twenty. The ground colour is an un- marked olive-brown.

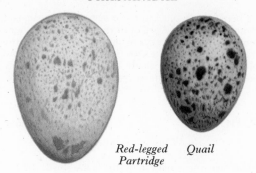

Red-legged   *Quail*
Partridge

RED-LEGGED PARTRIDGE   April-June
Alectoris rufa

Like Pheasants, Red-legged Partridges, in some districts called French Partridges, are not native birds
but have been brought here for sporting purposes.
Their introduction is much more recent, however,
as it took place towards the end of the eighteenth
century. They are not so common as Grey Partridges, and have a restricted distribution in the
British Isles, being largely confined to the midland
and south-eastern counties of England. Their
haunts are similar to those of their near relatives, but
they prefer chalky, sandy or stony waste land.

The nesting site is also similar to that of the commoner birds, being usually beneath a bush or in a
hedge-bottom, although high sites are sometimes
chosen, such as the top of a haystack. The nest itself is a hollow with a scanty lining of grass and dead
leaves.

There is only one clutch of eggs in the year, laid towards the end of April or during May. It contains from nine to twenty eggs, which are generally a little larger than those of the Grey Partridge. The ground colour is a variable shade of buff and bears fine specks, sometimes interspersed with larger spots, of reddish- or a darker brown.

QUAIL   May-June

Coturnix coturnix

Quails are the smallest of the game-birds in the British Isles and the only members of the family here which are not residents. They are scarce summer visitors from the end of April, leaving again during October, although a few at times may spend the winter here. They are usually widely distributed throughout the British Isles, but very locally, and their numbers vary from year to year, though they are always thinly and only locally distributed. They frequent open fields and waste land, particularly where there is plenty of cover.

This cover provides the site for the nest, which is a hollow scraped among grass and other plants and rather sparsely lined with a few wisps of grass.

Laying begins during May or sometimes as late as the beginning of June, and there is only one clutch in the year. It contains between seven and ten (occasionally more) eggs, which are somewhat variable. The ground colour is yellow or some shade of buff, and the markings are a rich brown or near-black. They consist of specks, spots and blotches scattered over the whole shell.

INDEX

213

INDEX

INDEX

INDEX

PRINTED BY
LOWE AND BRYDONE (PRINTERS) LTD., LONDON, N.W.10

570.554